THE GWR SWINDON TO BATH LINE

THE GWR SWINDON TO BATH LINE

COLIN G. MAGGS

SUTTON PUBLISHING

First published in the United Kingdom in 2003
Sutton Publishing Limited · Phoenix Mill · Stroud · Gloucestershire · GL5 2BU

British Library Cataloguing-in-Publication Data.
A record for this book is available from the British Library.

ISBN 0-7509-3403-4

Typeset in 11/13 pt Bembo.
Typesetting and origination by
Sutton Publishing Limited.
Printed and bound in Great Britain by
J.H. Haynes and Co. Ltd.

CONTENTS

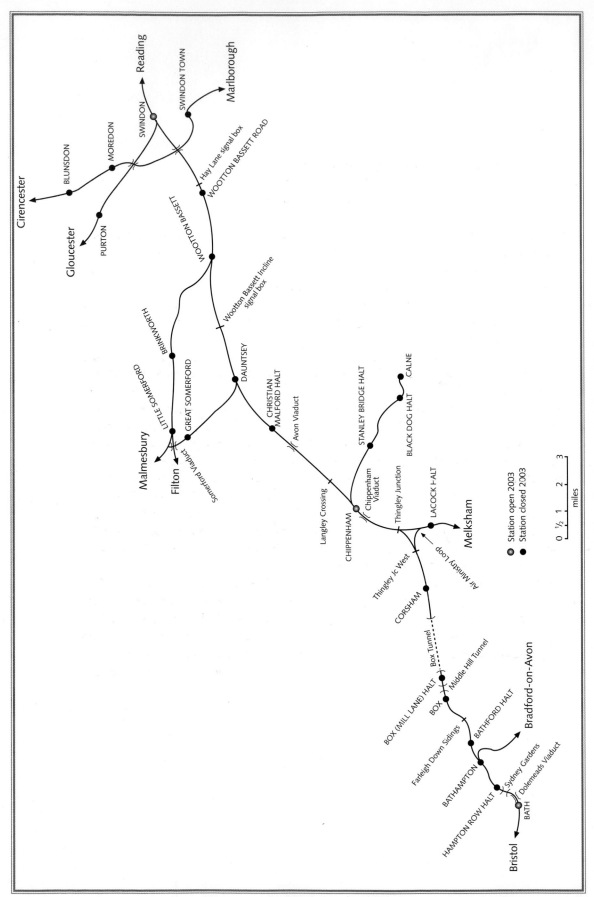

Map of the railway between Swindon and Bath.

INTRODUCTION

The Swindon and Bath line was the last link of the Great Western Railway between London, Bath and Bristol. For hundreds of years a road had united these cities, but the Industrial Revolution brought the need for faster passenger transportation and created heavy commercial traffic unsuited to the roads of the late eighteenth and early nineteenth centuries. The Kennet & Avon Canal, opened in 1810, provided a partial solution, but the development of the steam railway engine in the 1820s provided a more efficient alternative.

The ideal concept of a railway held by Isambard Kingdom Brunel, the GWR's engineer, was a straight, level line. This was possible from Paddington to Swindon, the ruling gradient being 1 in 660, but he was then faced with a difficulty: Swindon lay about 300 ft above sea level and Bath 100 ft. His answer was two steep gradients of 1 in 100 worked by stationary steam engines, water power, or a line on the atmospheric principle. In the event, during the years between the line's planning and opening, locomotives were improved to such an extent that they proved capable of climbing such a gradient.

As the railway system was extended, the Swindon to Bath line became part of the route to Exeter, Plymouth and Penzance, and, with the opening of the Severn Tunnel in 1886, to South Wales. By 1906 the volume of traffic between Swindon and Bristol was eased by the opening of a new, shorter route to the west via Newbury, Lavington and Somerton, while the Severn Tunnel was reached by the Bristol & South Wales Direct Railway curving from the Bath line at Wootton Bassett.

Despite the opening of the M4, giving a fast road alternative to the railway, traffic congestion in London and its approaches means that rail travel is still extremely viable, especially with the introduction in 1976 of High Speed Trains (HSTs), bringing Bath to within just over an hour of the capital. In recent years Swindon has grown in size, and far from being a small market town on a hill a mile from the railway, has become a large conurbation with a population of some 180,000, creating considerable daily passenger traffic by rail.

Transport in pre-railway days: a horse wagon which operated between Bath and Bristol.

(Author's Collection)

ACKNOWLEDGEMENTS

Grateful acknowledgement for assistance is due to: R. Ball, G. Brown, A. Cannings, W. Croom, Dr A.J.G. Dickens, E. Francis, C. Hancock, N. Hitchcock, R. Jones, J. Mann, P. Mortimore, F. Nash, C. Roberts, W. Talbot, R. Walker and N. Whalley. Especial thanks are due to E.J.M. Hayward for checking and improving the manuscript.

Chapter One

PLANNING & CONSTRUCTION

The first proposal for a Bristol to London line was from the London & Bristol Rail Road Company in 1824. One of the directors was the road engineer John Loudon McAdam. He was appointed engineer to the project which was to run via Mangotsfield, Wootton Bassett, Wantage and Reading, but the scheme was aborted.

However, encouraged by the success of the Stockton & Darlington Railway, opened in 1825, fifteen Bristol citizens representing five public bodies – Bristol Corporation; the Society of Merchant Venturers; the Bristol Dock Company; the Bristol Chamber of Commerce; and the Bristol and Gloucestershire Railway – met on 21 January 1833 to investigate the possibility of building a railway to London. Brunel, aged twenty-seven, was appointed as engineer. East of Bath he had two options by which to reach Reading: via Bradford-on-Avon and the Vale of Pewsey, or by way of Swindon and the Vale of the White Horse. He recommended the latter.

A detailed report was presented to a public meeting at the Guildhall, Bristol, on 30 July 1833 and it was resolved that

a Company should be formed for the establishment of Railway communication between Bristol and London, and for that purpose a body of Directors for Bristol be appointed, who, in conjunction with a similar body to be appointed in London, shall constitute a General Board of Management for securing subscriptions and obtaining an Act of Parliament for effecting the same object.

The first joint meeting of the two committees was held in Messrs Gibbs' counting house, Lime Street, London, on 19 August 1833, when the title 'Great Western Railway' was adopted. It was preferred to the alternative 'Bristol & London Railroad' because it was believed that as Bristol's trade may have been thought to be declining in favour of Liverpool, having Bristol in the title might raise apprehension among investors.

The scheme first came before the Parliamentary Committee on 16 April 1834, and on the fifty-seventh day of the hearing the committee approved it and it passed the Commons with 182 votes for and 92 against. However, the Lords rejected it on 25 July 1834 by 47 to 30, so the scheme, which an opposing counsel described as neither 'great' nor 'western', or even a 'railway', temporarily fell into abeyance.

GWR supporters drummed up backing all over the West of England and South Wales, and in 1835 another application was made to Parliament. Chief opposition came from the London & Southampton Railway, which was promoting a Basingstoke, Bath & Bristol Railway, but on 26 May 1835 the GWR Bill passed the Lords on a vote of 49 to 27, the bill receiving royal assent on 31 August 1835.

Some people imagined problems with Box Tunnel; a contributor to the *Bath Chronicle* in May 1835 wrote: 'Consider the confined unwholesome air of the tunnel, which would be ventilated by no upright shaft, and the temperature would be that of a well!!

To the Right Honorable the LORDS, Spiritual and Temporal, of the United Kingdom of Great Britain and Ireland, in Parliament assembled.

The humble PETITION of the undersigned Merchants, Bankers, Manufacturers, Traders, and Inhabitants of the CITY of BRISTOL,

SHEWETH,

That your Petitioners have viewed with the deepest interest the progress of a Bill in your Right Honourable House for making a Railway from Bristol to London, to be called "*The Great Western Railway*."

That a very large portion of the Inhabitants of this city have invested their Money in that undertaking from a conviction of the Public Benefits that would arise from it, and in the fullest confidence that the very best means have been adopted to secure the completion of that Measure in the manner best calculated to promote their Interests and those of the Public generally.

That your Petitioners are informed and believe that a Rival Company, with whom they have no sort of connexion, have been the principal if not the only Opponents of the Great Western Railway Bill in Parliament, with a view to compel the promoters of that measure to adopt another and an inferior Line in connexion with the Southampton Railway, and for the mere purpose of increasing the value of that speculation.

That your Petitioners most humbly submit that the Southampton Railway Company can have no right whatever to interfere with the efforts of the City of Bristol, which have been repeated during two Sessions of Parliament, from a conviction of their claim to the legislative sanction, and which during two successive Parliaments have actually received the sanction of the Lower House.

That if the Great Western Railway be again defeated, your Petitioners are well satisfied they shall altogether be deprived of the benefits of a Railway, as there are no Funds for the completion of any other undertaking that has been suggested in opposition to it, nor could your Petitioners ever venture to support such undertaking while convinced of the superiority of the one they are advocating, and in which they have Invested Capital to a large extent.

That the benefits of a Railway Communication between Bristol and London will be thus unnecessarily retarded to the manifest prejudice of Bristol, which must be placed in a position of very inferior advantage to Liverpool, between which place and London a Railway has already received the Legislative sanction.

That South Wales and Ireland (particularly the Southern part) will also be deprived of the benefits anticipated from a Railway Communication between Bristol and London, to the great prejudice of their Inhabitants, many of whom are Subscribers to a considerable amount.

Your Petitioners therefore earnestly implore your Lordships not to suffer the true Interests of Bristol, and of the Public, to be sacrificed to the efforts of a speculative Company, having no connexion with, or interest in, the City of Bristol, and having, in fact, no other object in view than their own pecuniary Profit.

And your Petitioners, as in duty bound, will ever pray, &c.

The above Petition lies for SIGNATURE, at

The Railroad Office - - Corn-Street.
The Commercial Rooms -   ditto.
At Gutch and Martin's! - Small-Street.

An 1835 petition to the House of Lords to accept the GWR bill.

(Author's Collection)

The 1846 condition of Chippenham Viaduct west of the station.

(Engraving by J.C. Bourne)

Also the danger; the positive imminent risk of life – to say nothing of the minor evils of utter darkness and concentrated noise!!'

George Stephenson was one of the witnesses called by the GWR promoters. The counsel who cross-examined him remarked: 'The noise of two trains passing each other in this tunnel would shake the nerves of this assembly. I do not know such a noise. No passenger would be induced to go twice.'

G.E. Frere was appointed resident engineer to the Bristol end of the GWR, though Brunel seemed to delegate little responsibility as he continually dashed to and fro between the Bristol and London sections. The Bristol Committee had authority to act independently of its London counterpart and permitted a much greater expenditure on station buildings, architectural decorations, and ornamental works generally.

The section from Chippenham to Bath was by far the heaviest: a stone viaduct west of Chippenham station was followed by a high embankment 2 miles long, then 3 miles of deep cutting through Corsham to Box Tunnel, at the time the longest in the country at 3 miles. Half a mile beyond was Middle Hill Tunnel and a 3-mile-long embankment to Bathampton, including a substantial bridge over the Avon at Bathford. On the outskirts of Bath, the Kennet & Avon Canal had to be diverted and a tall, substantial retaining wall built to support it. For stopping boats while the diversion was made, the GWR had to pay the canal company £20 per hour for 383 hours, a total of £7,660. Beyond the canal diversion the railway passed through two short tunnels, then along an embankment and over a viaduct to Bath station.

A 1846 view westwards from Bathwick Hill, showing Dolemeads Viaduct and St James's Bridge.

(Engraving by J.C. Bourne)

CONTRACT FOR WORKS.
Great Western Railway, Bristol.

NOTICE is hereby given,—That the Directors will receive at their Office, in Bristol, on or before Monday, the 20th of MARCH next, at Twelve o'Clock, Tenders for the execution of the following Works.

CHIPPENHAM DIVISION.
CONTRACT No. 1, C.

The Excavation and Formation of the Earthwork, and the Construction of all Bridges, Culverts, and other Masonry, and the entire Completion (excepting the Ballasting, and laying the permanent Rails) of that portion of the Railway extending from the East end of the Box Tunnel to the boundary of the fields, Nos. 18 and 19, Chippenham, a distance of about four miles and fifty chains.

This Contract consists principally of heavy Cutting and Embankment, and comprehends a large amount of Earthwork.

Drawings and Specifications of the above Works will be exhibited at the Company's Offices, Corn Street, Bristol, and at Hanwell, near London ; and printed Forms of Tender may be had at the same Offices, on and after Tuesday, the 28th inst.

The Directors will not consider themselves bound to accept the lowest Tender ; and they expect the several parties to attend at the Office, Corn Street, Bristol, at One o'Clock on Monday, the 20th of March.

C. A. SAUNDERS, ⎱ *Secretaries.*
I. J. CHAPMAN, ⎰

Corn Street, Bristol ; 1st Feb. 1837.   [8277

An advertisement inviting tenders for the construction of bridges, culverts and other masonry from the east end of the Box Tunnel, 21 February 1837 (*Bath & Cheltenham Gazette*).

(Author's Collection)

GREAT WESTERN RAILWAY.
Contract for Works.

NOTICE IS HEREBY GIVEN,—That the Directors will receive at their Office, CORN STREET, BRISTOL, on or before 12 o'Clock, FRIDAY, the 14th of FEBRUARY, TENDERS for the Construction of the following WORKS:

1. STONE BRIDGE across the River Avon, and VIADUCT in the Dolemeads, at Bath.
2. BRIDGE across the Pulteney Road, Bath.

The Company have secured a Quarry for the Supply of Stone, which the Contractors will have the option of working.

3. A BRIDGE in STONE or BRICK, across the River Avon, near Christian Malford.

Drawings and Specifications will be exhibited at the Company's Office, CLAVERTON STREET, BATH, where printed Forms of Tender may be had on and after TUESDAY, the 28th Inst.

The Directors will not consider themselves bound to accept the lowest Tender ; and they expect the several parties to attend at the Office, Corn Street, Bristol, at One o'Clock on the 14th Feb.

C. A. SAUNDERS, } SECRETARIES.
THOMAS OSLER,   }

Corn Street, Bristol; 23d Jan. 1840.   ⌐4410

An advertisement to tender for building bridges at Bath and Christian Malford, 4 February 1840 (*Bath & Cheltenham Gazette*).

(*Author's Collection*)

Work started on the section between Chippenham and Box Tunnel in the summer of 1837, but two years later the work was only half finished, the wet winter of 1839 having caused landslips.

The GWR usually offered landowners a fair price for their property. An inquiry was held on 19 September 1837 at the White Lion Hotel, Bath to assay the value of three houses in Bathwick Terrace required by the railway. The company offered £2,700; Mackay, the owner, claimed £3,200; and the jury's verdict was £2,650! The line passed under Bathwick Terrace, which had to be almost entirely rebuilt.

The contracts for building the line from Shrivenham to Chippenham were let in the spring of 1839, but work was delayed by the wet winter. Matters were straightforward as far as milepost 80¼, where Hay Lane crossed at the beginning of the long Studley Cutting. However, the section westwards from Hay Lane to Chippenham offered problems. Four cuttings were required with a maximum depth of 40–50 ft, plus three embankments 30–40 ft high, and another of 20 ft, but 3¾ miles in length. By October 1839 works extended from the eastern portal of Box Tunnel almost to Christian Malford, about 8 miles.

The bridge over the Avon at Christian Malford gave Brunel trouble and work was delayed by frost. To try to avoid slips, Brunel endeavoured not to make embankments during wet weather. Nevertheless, two near Wootton Bassett caused difficulties, and in February 1840 Brunel reported to his Board:

At Chippenham the works have proceeded well, but in the neighbourhood of Wootton Bassett such have been the effects of the weather that it is probable that time and expense might have been ultimately saved by totally suspending the works during the last autumn and winter.

The quantity of work done during this period has been so limited that it would have required a few weeks only of summer weather to form the same extent of earthwork in a more substantial manner without incurring the same risk of future delays in the progress of the contracts from the slipping of earth excavated and thrown into embankment in a wet state. Arrangements are now making for redeeming as far as possible the time which has been lost, by prosecuting the works by the use of locomotive engines and other means with every possible vigour and despatch during the coming season.

Six months later he resorted to side cutting to obtain material for wider embankments. As the material was immediately to hand, it 'has not only improved the quality of the earthwork, but has enabled me to expedite the final completion, and at the same time to perform the great bulk of the work during the Summer instead of the Winter months'. The longitudinal pits caused by the side cutting, near the foot of the embankment, are today water-filled. However, the wider embankments did not solve Brunel's problem of slipping embankments, so in the spring of 1841, in order to complete the work, he tried driving piles down each side of the embankment into solid ground and lashing the tops of the piles together with chains. Even this failed to solve the problem as the clay continued to move, and a slip at the foot of Wootton Bassett incline on 7 September 1841 derailed the Down Mail.

The contract for building the line between Box and Bath was not let until May 1839. In September navvies commenced work at Hampton Row excavating a new bed for the Kennet & Avon Canal, as its old site was required for the railway. The *Bath Chronicle* of 12 November 1839 reported: 'Nearly all the soil necessary for turning the canal has been removed and used on the railway; about 100 yards of the inclined plane leading to it, having been finished. At Hampton and in the fields beyond, the cuttings and embankments are in a forward state.' The same issue of the paper carried an advertisement for tendering to build St James's Bridge, and on 16 January 1840 to

St James's Bridge view upstream, 25 June 1979.

(C.G. Maggs)

construct the Dolemeads Viaduct. On 30 April 1840 the *Bath Chronicle* reported that the fine weather had enabled the contractor to make up time on the Wootton Bassett to Swindon section; that the erection of Dolemeads Viaduct had started; as well as the cutting of the tunnel at Raby Place near Sydney Gardens. In mid-May 1840 the works at Wootton Bassett were 'spiritedly carried forward'. Construction at Bathampton revealed three skeletons of soldiers killed during the Civil War, one with a 3½ lb cannonball in his chest. As the directors were anxious for the line to be opened, contractors were given 'liberal offers' to finish works well within their contract time.

On 15 November 1840 a great slip occurred on the railway close to the canal at Hampton Row, leaving so narrow an embankment between the canal and the railway works below that Brunel requested that water be immediately let out of the canal to enable the works to be secured to prevent a further accident.

A serious flood on 16 January 1841 caused more problems. A temporary wooden bridge across the Avon at Bathford, erected for the convenience of railway workmen, floated 'with great violence' down the river towards St James's Bridge. The abutments of the latter had been erected, massive piles driven deep into the river bed, strong centrings fixed, and all was ready for masons to build the arch. The flood swept the temporary bridge at Bathford downstream until it struck the centrings of St James's Bridge with a tremendous impact and carried them away. A large mass of woodwork was carried down the river, some lodging against the railway skew bridge west of Bath station, while the rest formed a partial dam at the Old Bridge, where the debris was secured by ropes and chains. The episode cost Chadwick, the contractor, £1,000. A large quantity of tools belonging to artisans at work on St James's Bridge was also lost, and the loss would have been greater had work not been temporarily suspended because of the frost.

Brunel's half-yearly report, given on 25 February 1841, said that in the immediate neighbourhood of Bath much needed to be done, but that the high canal retaining wall at Hampton Row was almost complete. He believed that following the canal's diversion, railway construction would be 'a simple and easy operation'. Bathford Bridge was in arrears, but works from there to Box were in a forward state and the surface was being prepared for ballasting. Middle Hill Tunnel and its cuttings on either side were almost finished and the Wootton Bassett contract nearly complete. Works between Chippenham and Box were on schedule. In April 1841 preparations were being made for erecting Chippenham station in a field called Wall Ground, its entrance being through the once-extensive timber yard of John Provis.

On Saturday night, 3 April 1841, workmen began the operation of diverting the canal at Hampton Row to its new channel, and work continued the next day. Morris Perry, a railway labourer, was summoned by the Lord's Day Observance Society for working on Sunday. Melmoth Waters, for the LDOS, said that the intention was not to deal harshly with him, but rather to secure a day of rest for workmen. Henry and William Oldham, the contractors who employed between fifty and sixty men on the task, were also charged. The defendants were fined 5s costs. The contractors tried to avoid Sunday labour, but this was not always possible. For example, on 2 May 1841 navvies were seen at work near Sydney Gardens. The 'respectable contractor' said that he purposely left the work on Saturday so that nothing needed to be done until Monday, but on Sunday he was ordered by GWR agents to set men to work and was told that if he did not comply, they would give the necessary order.

The centrings of St James's Bridge were removed in mid-May 1841 and the permanent way laid between Bathampton and Bathford. 'Large crowds are daily to be seen on the

Permanent-way gangers, Sydney Gardens, 1846, view Down.

(Engraving by J.C. Bourne)

banks of the canal, and other parts commanding a view of the works near Sydney Gardens, which are progressing with extraordinary rapidity', reported the *Bath & Cheltenham Gazette* of 25 May 1841. Bath station was also nearing completion: only a temporary structure had been used for the opening of the Bristol to Bath line on 31 August 1840.

NAVVIES

Many navvies earned 4*s* a day and some 8*s*, which were very good wages when compared with those of agricultural labourers, who only received 9 to 12*s* a week, or 15*s* when working overtime in spring. Navvies, being relatively affluent and probably living away from home, often spent their free time drinking, sometimes to excess, and this caused problems. Churches tried to cater for their needs. On Sunday afternoons the navvies' chaplain, the Revd W.C. Osborn, held services at the Railway Episcopal Chapel, Batheaston, situated in the Old Poor House just east of Five Ways. About 150 navvies attended on 3 May 1840, when they were recorded as being 'extremely attentive to the prayers'. Mr Osborn also held services on Thursday evenings in the schoolroom near the church at Box, and in 1840 the south aisle was added to the parish church to accommodate the workmen.

On 26 January 1840 a sermon was preached in St Saviour's Church, Bath, in aid of a fund 'to ameliorate the destitute spiritual condition of the men working on the rail-road'.

On 19 October 1840, forty men and boys employed building the railway at Bathford and Box gathered with the Mr Osborn to eat supper in the room under the Episcopal Chapel, Batheaston: 'Some resident engineers and gentlemen were present and ministered to the comfort of the men.' A Railwaymen's Christmas Festival was held on 25 December 1840, the men eating beef, drinking coffee and attending a service at the Railway Chapel, Batheaston. The event was organised 'to restrain men from using the beer houses in the village'.

Some of the contractors were caring. For example, Messrs Lewis and Brewer, who had the contract for the east end of Box Tunnel, persuaded their men to contribute to a fund which paid the sick 1s a day, and those who had met with accident, 1s 6d each.

Some navvies had a solitary existence outside work. Norris, employed in making the cutting at Corsham, was found dead on 1 December 1838 in the hay loft of the Rail Road Inn (now the Great Western) in Pound Pill. He had slept there for some time and been unwell for two or three days before his death.

Coping with alcohol was the navvies' main problem. On 18 August 1839 William Vickers, a Devonian, entered the taproom of the Chequers Inn near Corsham, and drank beer, ginger beer, and then a considerable quantity of gin. He was placed in the outer room and a few hours later was found dead 'of apoplexy occasioned by excessive drinking'.

Some navvies found accommodation in local cottages and inns, but the field next to the Quakers' burial ground near the Batheaston/Bathford parish boundary was covered with sheds to house navvies and horses. *The Bath & County Graphic* of October 1899, recalling events of sixty years before, reported:

Making a cutting at Corsham, 1841.

(*G. Childs*)

A footbridge crossed the river from it, over which was an endless stream of barrows, men going and returning, wheeling materials for the bridge. Every cottage was overcrowded with navvies. Scenes of disorder and fights were not unusual, a favourite spot for the latter being the meadow through which the footpath passes to the river side. Here, sometimes, three or four battles royal were going on at the same time. The old Squire (he must have been a young man then, but he was always called 'old' on account of his grey hair), was a little man, but game as a terrier and he would go in between these brawny athletes and separate them, threatening them with all sorts of legal disasters if they did not desist. He never got hurt – the men seemed to recognise his pluck.

The United Hospital ('Royal' was not added until 23 May 1864) in Bath had to treat many injured navvies, the line between Swindon and Bath causing an above-average number of accidents, and these did not only occur in Box Tunnel.

On 15 May 1838 John Bancroft, from Bradford-on-Avon, was working in the cutting near Corsham when earth fell unexpectedly. He saw it moving, but unfortunately his escape route was blocked by a tram wagon. Almost 3 tons of earth fell on his legs, fracturing both. He received immediate attention from Dr Little, surgeon to the works. Two days later, John Howel of Kingston St Michael, an 'aged man', was fatally crushed by an earth fall. The *Bath Chronicle* commented that accidents which occurred on railway construction generally happened to those whose permanent home was in the neighbourhood and who therefore were comparatively unaccustomed to the work. Up to 24 May 1838 it recorded that '13 men have now lost their lives in the vicinity'.

On 4 August 1838 a young man known as 'Clockline' received a fractured jaw when endeavouring to stop an empty wagon descending an inclined plane on the ballast heap at Thingley by spragging a wheel. He failed to carry out the operation skilfully, as the stick was carried round by the wheel and struck him in the face. He was seen by Dr Little 'and is fast recovering'. Two more accidents happened at Thingley about the same time. A boy, Isaac Horne, was playing with gunpowder and it exploded, small stones cutting his face. In another incident, Sailor Jack had prepared a shot for firing and imprudently used gunpowder instead of touch paper to ignite it. Unsurprisingly it exploded before he could leave for safety. He was blasted about 15 ft into the air. Spectators expected to find him dead and were amazed to see him get up and run away with just a bruised ankle. Thingley was certainly a dangerous place.

In May 1839 Mr Hobbs of Lacock was crushed to death when earth slipped near the end of Corsham cutting. 'His bones were broken in a dreadful manner. He left a wife and family to lament his untimely death.'

On 14 February 1839, at Patterdown, near Chippenham, Hood, a lad in charge of a horse drawing a train of spoil wagons to form an embankment, slipped and the wagons passed over and severed his leg, killing him. Similarly, on 8 October 1839 another boy, William Olive, slipped and a wagon cut off his foot at the instep. He was taken to Chippenham workhouse for amputation. He recovered from the operation and returned to his family at Lacock. On 6 May 1840 a boy at Wootton Bassett slipped and a loaded wagon ran over him, almost severing his leg from his body. The paper, not glossing over anything, reported that Hooper, the doctor in attendance, 'gives no hope of his recovery'. The boy, with another lad, had escaped from Banbury Workhouse a few weeks previously. The following month William Gough, in trying to stop a contractor's tram wagon, fell across the rails. It passed over his foot, which was later amputated at Chippenham Workhouse.

On 6 August 1840 John Allen was working by the canal at Hampton Row when he slipped, fell and a whole train of tram wagons ran over his right arm and thigh. Loss of blood caused his death soon after his arrival at the United Hospital, Bath. His funeral on Sunday 9 August in Bathwick churchyard was attended by a large crowd of his fellow workers. 'The men were all uniformly dressed in clean smock frocks, and each wore a white bow in his hat. A few of them appeared to be deeply affected by the calamitous accident', reported the *Bath Chronicle*.

This proved to be the first of several accidents in the area that month. On 7 August John Dingle was crushed at Bathford by falling earth. Carried to the United Hospital, he lingered until the 9th. On 11 August a fatal accident occurred to William Atkins, aged fifteen, when a train of loaded wagons between Bathford and Middle Hill moved unexpectedly and passed over both thighs. On 22 August, at Dolemeads Viaduct, as a piece of timber was being hauled up, a portion of scaffolding gave way and 'the whole mass fell with a frightful crash'. Unfortunately, George Matthews was passing under the arch and the heavy beam struck his head, 'which was so frightfully shattered by the blow that not a vestige of his features could be distinguished'. He left a wife and four young children. On 26 August earth fell on two labourers near Middle Hill, killing one outright while the other, with a broken thigh, was taken to the United Hospital. The final fatal accident occurred at Cocklebury, Chippenham, on the 27th. A man had incautiously undermined the earth too far and it fell on him.

September was a rather safer month. Only Wood and Greedy, working near Sydney Gardens, were injured by falling earth. Greedy remained buried for such a long time that he was feared dead, but he was eventually rescued suffering just a dislocated hip. Wood's thigh bone was broken.

On 6 October Henry Bladon was wheeling earth up one of the horse runs on a cutting east of Chippenham when the chain to which the barrow was attached broke. He was thrown to the ground from a height of 25 ft, the barrow falling with him. He was fortunate indeed that no bones were broken. In mid-October John Tapp was sawing stone for Dolemeads Viaduct when a box containing stones being drawn up, fell and injured him so gravely that he died half an hour after being admitted to the United Hospital.

An accident due to intoxication occurred on 6 February 1841. John Simpson, aged twenty-five, a railway labourer, slept for warmth by a limekiln near the skew bridge carrying what is now the A420 over the line west of Wootton Bassett. In his sleep he was burnt to death and a wheelbarrow, placed nearby to shelter him from the wind, was, apart from its ironwork, reduced to ashes.

On 10 April 1841, Stafford, 'of steady and industrious habits', was at work in the cutting near the eastern mouth of Box Tunnel when a large stone dislodged by blasting fell on his head, 'and so injured him that he lasted only a few hours'.

At Cocklebury, Chippenham, on 23 May 1841 several men had just loaded a railway wagon with sleepers and had mounted the unroped load when the horses attached set off at full speed. The wagon hit an obstruction, with the result that sleepers and men were thrown off. One was taken to the nearby Black Horse Inn, but the surgeon said his thigh was only bruised, not broken. Three days later, between 3 and 4 a.m., Joseph Walker, aged twelve, was driving a horse and tramway wagon at Wootton Bassett when he fell on the rail. Both wheels passed over his body and 'nearly cut him asunder'.

On 21 June 1841 John Hewitt was at work near Sydney Gardens, Bath, under a plank stretched across the line. When another labourer passed over it, an end fell on Hewitt's head, fracturing his skull and jaw. He was taken to the United Hospital and died on

5 July in a state of delirium. The inquest brought in a verdict of accidental death and a deodand of 1s was placed on the plank. He left a wife and three children.

In the *Report of the Select Committee on Railway Labourers*, published in 1846, Brunel listed 131 navvies, not including those slightly injured, who had been taken to the Bath United Hospital between 30 September 1839 and 24 June 1841. He commented: 'I think it is a small list considering the very heavy works and the immense amount of powder used, and some of the heaviest and most difficult works; I am afraid it does not show the whole extent of accidents incurred in the district.' He was asked again if he did not think the list startling and repeated he did not. The number of accidents he believed small considering so many men had been at work for two or three years.

Fights and robberies were other activities indulged in by navvies. On Sunday 20 August 1837 John Awdry, a magistrate of Reybridge Cottage, Lacock, remonstrated with a gang of railway labourers for their 'impropriety of conduct'. In reply they violently assaulted him. The offenders were caught and sent to Devizes prison. On 22 January 1838 Mr Manley, of the Roebuck Inn, Lacock Road, Corsham, observed a railway labourer leaving his house, having stolen the kitchen fire irons. Manley took the tongs from him and was struck over the head with a poker. The thief was taken into custody and in default of payment of the fine spent two months in the 'Devizes house of correction'.

Mid-November 1839 saw a fight lasting several hours at Christian Malford between rival gangs of navvies. It was immediately prior to the setting up of a county police force which the inhabitants were anxiously awaiting to protect them from such riots. In December 1839 the contractor working at Christian Malford was declared bankrupt and this caused suffering to several poor village tradesmen. On 15 February 1840 navvies at Sutton Benger made an unprovoked attack on a passing carter and this escalated into a fight between labourers and villagers, the latter aided by the new police force. Some windows were also smashed. The ringleaders were caught and appeared before magistrates. The value of the police was demonstrated because on previous occasions the villagers had been completely at the mercy of the rioters.

Workmen sometimes entered into a legal dispute with a contractor. For instance, at Bath on 19 May 1841 John Clewitt, railway contractor, was summoned by Arthur Hobbs, mason, to show why he refused to pay him 6s 6d arrears of wages. Hobbs had been engaged to work for Clewitt on the railway works at Hampton Row at 4s 6d a day, but Clewitt, on paying the wages, refused to give him more than 4s a day. The defendant was required to pay the deficiency and costs.

BOX TUNNEL

At 1 mile 1,452 yd long and burrowing through the southern ranges of the Cotswold Hills, Box Tunnel is the major engineering feature of the Swindon to Bath line, and was 800 yd longer than any other tunnel built prior to the 1840s. The width of land enclosed for the tunnel was 30 ft, and on completion of the work it was returned to its owners, subject to right of way to the shafts. The tunnel was made using eight shafts numbered from west to east, the first and last of which were enlarged into cuttings for the entrances, so that only six remained. One of them was subsequently blocked, leaving five remaining today.

Work started early in 1836, sinking trial shafts to ascertain the nature of the ground. On 13 June 1836 Brunel reported to his directors:

Navvies cutting a tunnel heading.

(F.W. Simms)

Five temporary shafts have been sunk on the line of the tunnel to various depths varying from 40 feet to 90 feet to determine the position of the strata of the Oolite through which all of them have been carried – a sixth has been found necessary at the west end – before I can determine with sufficient certainty the exact position of the clay and Fullers' Earth which lies under the Oolite and the proportionate length of the tunnel which it will pass through must govern the relative distance of the permanent shafts – this remaining shaft will be worked day and night and as soon as the required information is obtained which I hope will be in a fortnight, we shall be able to prepare and to let the contracts of these permanent shafts which I propose to do separately from the Tunnel in order that the materials through which each portion of the latter is to be carried may be ascertained and worked by the parties most accustomed to the particular description of material and not contracted for blindly on a mere speculation.

I am, gentlemen, your most obedient servant,
I.K. Brunel

In November 1836, under the supervision of Charles Richardson, later responsible for the Severn Tunnel, six permanent and two temporary shafts each 28 ft in diameter were bored from the surface to the planned level of the line. All the shafts, varying from 70 to 300 ft in depth, were completed by the autumn of 1837 and the tunnel contracts advertised. Following the plan outlined in the last sentence of the above letter, George Burge of Herne Bay, then building St Katherine's Dock in London, won the contract for cutting three-quarters of the tunnel through clay, blue marl and inferior oolite. The remaining ½ mile was cut by Brewer of Box and Lewis of Bath, who had the necessary skill for working with great oolite and had already sunk trial shafts for this portion. Both contracts stipulated that the work was to be finished in thirty months, that is, by August 1840, and for a defined monthly progress to be kept. The *Bath & Cheltenham Gazette* of 27 February 1838 commented:

Navvies deepening a tunnel heading.

(F.W. Simms)

The Directors we think did wisely in giving the contractors such ample means of ascertaining the nature of the materials they have to encounter, as they have thus been able to secure the completion of work on terms closely corresponding with the Engineer's estimate, and not influenced by the exaggerated apprehension of difficulties which ignorance of the strata might create.

Work on the tunnel itself had started in December 1837. The costs in Burge's contract were:

	£	s	d
Driving the tunnel, exclusive of masonry or brickwork per cu. yd		10	6
Brickwork set in mortar, including costs of scaffolding, etc. per cu. yd	2	3	6
Ditto set in Roman cement	2	8	6
Coursed rubble set in mortar, including scaffolding, etc. per cu. yd		18	6
Ditto set in Roman cement	1	1	6
Ashlar set in mortar, including scaffolding, etc. per cu. ft		1	0½
Ditto set in Roman cement		1	2½

Burge, cutting through ground which needed supporting, probably used the 'English method' perfected by canal-builders fifty years earlier. First a pilot heading was driven along what became the tunnel arch. Crown bars were inserted, supported at one end by the brick lining and at the other on timber props. Miners would then widen and deepen the excavation supported by timber. Larch bars were preferred as they gave an audible creak if the load was excessive and collapse imminent; this could then be forestalled with extra props. Clay swelled on exposure and could exert a considerable force. In Box Tunnel

6 in were allowed for the clay's expansion between the face of the work and timbers. Behind the excavators came bricklayers who added a lining. At no point were unlined excavations more than about 8 ft ahead of the bricklayers. Approximately 5,500 bricks were needed for every foot advanced.

In June 1838 miners and bricklayers were actively engaged on the east and west faces of shafts Nos 2, 3, 4 and 5, the most laborious and difficult part of the tunnel. At Nos 7 and 8 the headings were proceeding 'with considerable perseverance', as they had to contend with the influx of an immense volume of water from surrounding springs. Hundreds of hogsheads (50 gallons) were drawn off daily from No. 7 by a steam engine working day and night, yet more than 20 ft of water remained.

A ton of gunpowder and a ton of candles, the latter made at Box, were consumed each week, with the gunpowder being mainly for blasting rock and perhaps some hard clays. The holes for blasting were made by hand-held steel drills, a hammerman striking while the holder-up would rotate the drill after each end strike. Relays of small boys, called tool carriers, ran to and from the blacksmith as the drills needed resharpening after penetrating about 2 ft.

Blasting was dangerous, the *Wiltshire Independent* recording:

A few weeks ago, a man was about to 'fire a shot', that is, to blow up a piece of rock: he had prepared the hole for the charge, and was in the act of pouring gunpowder into it from an iron canister, containing about 20 pounds, which he held under his arm, when a drop of water having fallen from the roof upon the wick of his candle – most imprudently placed close by the hole – a spark flew from it into the powder, causing a most terrific explosion. The canister was burst to atoms, but not one piece entered the unfortunate man who held it; he was dreadfully scorched, his clothes were torn off, his hair and eyebrows completely destroyed and his skin burned off all round his body; but his eyesight was uninjured, and, although from the action of the flames he was miserably wounded and disfigured, he is now in a fair way of recovery.

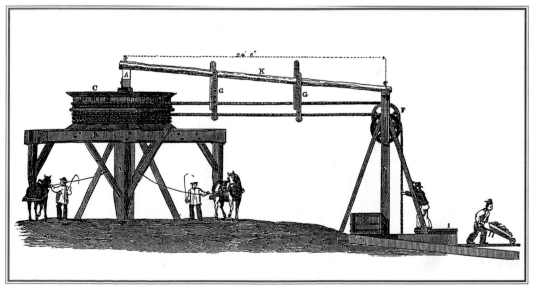

A horse gin used to raise or lower men and materials in the shaft on the right.

(F.W. Simms)

A busy scene near the head of a shaft.

F.W. Simms)

On 6 July 1839, at No. 4 shaft, a Mr Falkin approached a fuse, unaware that it was lit, and the stone in the succeeding explosion 'cut his head dreadfully'. Bickford's patent fuse was used when blasting stone. The cost of blasting freestone was approximately 5.87*d* per yard. In red sandstone 2½ lb of powder was used, but in freestone only 1 lb was required per cubic yard.

Workmen lodged in neighbouring villages, and because work went on night and day, no bed was ever cold – in fact, they played very appropriately 'Box & Cox'. In June 1839, following an application by some landowners and inhabitants, seventeen special constables were appointed under the Act of 1 & 2 Vic cap 80, which permitted payment to special constables to keep the peace 'near public works'. These constables were provided and paid for by the GWR.

By the end of August 1839 1,350 yd of tunnel had been excavated and almost 1,200 yd completely finished. Six months later, despite an ingress of water, 1,900 yd, or nearly two-thirds of the whole, had been completed. To expedite work, three extra shafts were sunk, opening six additional faces for excavation. Progress was at the rate of about 6 ft a day. Some 10 miners were employed at each heading, plus 6 fillers, totalling about 500 men working day and night. Daily wages for Burge's workers were:

Bricklayers	6s 0d
Miners	5s–5s 6d
Labourers	3s 6d

Miners working in freestone, which offered rather more pleasant conditions, were paid 3s 6d–4s, while their labourers were paid 3s.

Burge's section of the tunnel needed lining throughout and bricks were provided by Hunt's brickyard, employing 100 men in the meadows west of Chippenham at Lowden Hill, on the site of the present Kingham Close. For three years 100 horses and carts carried a total of 30 million bricks to the site. The bricks cost £2 1s 6d per 1,000.

James Martin, a young native of Corsham and carter for John May of the Hare and Hounds Inn, Pickwick, was employed conveying bricks from Hunt's kilns to one of the shafts of Box Tunnel. On Saturday 23 May 1840, anxious to arrive at the brickyard early to obtain his load first, he drove rather furiously and, seated on the shaft of his wagon, when it passed over a heap of stone in the road he fell off and both wheels passed over his body. He only survived about three hours.

Bricking a tunnel.

(F.W. Simms)

Brickwork consisted of seven rings, a half-brick in thickness; the arch of six rings; and the invert four rings. Ashes from Trowbridge formed the main component for mortar, and cement was supplied by Bailey & White of London. A large quantity of sand was dug about 2 miles from the tunnel and mixed with other ingredients to form other mortar. A limekiln on Box Hill continuously burnt lime from stones raised from the excavation. Burge's section was drier and he only required a steam pump at one shaft.

Lewis and Brewer's section was to be left unlined but the inrush of water through fissures in the Bath stone hampered work, especially in winter. In November 1837 water overpowered the pump, filled the tunnel workings and rose 56 ft up the shafts. Work had to be suspended until July 1838, when a second 50 hp pump was installed and working. The following November excess water again held up work, and on shafts Nos 6, 7 and 8 only a few men could work owing to water in the shafts, but the problem was overcome in less than a fortnight. Stothert & Pitt, the Bath engineers, manufactured the steam pumps.

Most of the work on the tunnel was done by horse and manual labour. Horse gins raised spoil and lowered material. A shaft had two gins driven by three horses, with a brakesman and two tippers in attendance. A total of 247,000 cubic yards of spoil were wound up the shafts. Burge employed 1,100–1,200 men and 100 horses.

Shaft No. 6 had two steam engines, one of 6 hp for raising and lowering material, and the other of 30 hp for working an 18-in-diameter pump to extract water from the tunnel. Lewis and Brewer had shafts Nos 7 and 8. No. 7 had three engines, two for pumping and a third for lifting. These engines used a total of 30 tons of coal each week, at a cost of £1 6s per ton. At No. 8 shaft an 8-hp engine powered two 8-in pumps and also raised and lowered materials. In most tunnels water could normally be lifted in barrels by horse gin.

The *Bath Chronicle* for 22 April 1837 reported:

Progress on the 7 permanent shafts is more than half complete. Two of the shallower shafts at the Chippenham end of the line are nearly completed and the rest have been sunk to a vertical depth of 150 ft. In proceeding with the deepest shafts, which will be 300 ft and carried through beds of forest marble, skallet, corn grit and ground stone, impediments have been overcome by the contractor arising from the great quantity of water draining through the joints in the oolite and settling on the division of strata in coming to the marl. To overcome these difficulties Brunel allowed some of his most skilled Thames Tunnel workmen to assist in Box Tunnel, the local men having been found more experienced in quarrying, rather than tunnelling.

James Tunstall MD, in *Rambles about Bath & its Neighbourhood*, published in 1847, states that in 1839 'We descended in the workmen's "skid", covered with mud; immense blocks of stone lay in confused heaps; water dropped around; swarthy men were employed, some in laying the masonry, others in hewing the rocks; trucks lay in confused heaps, picturesquely lit by, here and there, a candle; whilst immense discharges, as of artillery, reverberated around.'

At the half-yearly meeting in August 1838 it was reported that the tunnel works were proceeding well: 'The monthly rate of progress required is determined on, and proportionate penalties are attached to the non-performance of the quantity. At one of the shafts these penalties have already been levied.' In May 1839 it was reported that half a mile of tunnel was completed and no difficulty had been experienced in keeping it free from water. Work through freestone had proceeded with greater rapidity than was required by the contract.

F.S. Williams, in *Our Iron Roads*, wrote:

On one occasion some of the directors of the Great Western Railway were inspecting the works at the Box tunnel, and several of them resolved to descend a shaft with Mr Brunel and one or two of the other engineers, who mentioned the incident to the writer. Accordingly all but one ensconced themselves in the tub provided for that purpose – he declined to accompany them. His friends rallied him for his want of courage, and one slyly suggested, 'Did your wife forbid you before you started?' A quiet nod in response intimated that the right nail had been struck, and the revelation was received with a merry laugh. But as the pilgrims found themselves slipping about a greasy, muddy tub, jolting and shaking as the horses stopped – by whose aid they were lowered – and how at length they were suspended some hundred and fifty feet from the bottom, till the blastings that had been prepared roared and reverberated through the 'long-drawn caverns', more than one of the party who had laughed before, wished that they had received a similar prohibition to that of their friend above, and that they had manifested an equal amount of marital docility.

In July 1839 a correspondent of the *Wiltshire Independent* related his more detailed experiences:

The descent, by Shaft No. 7, which is 136 feet deep, is effected on a platform, without any railing or other security on the sides, attached to a broad, flat rope wound and unwound by a steam engine, and is attended with no inconvenience (if the idea of a fall from giddiness, or from the breaking of the rope, be not allowed to intrude), except the hard bump with which your arrival at the bottom is announced to you.

On stepping from the platform, and escaping from the water which constantly drips from the aperture above, you find yourself in a temperature which should the day be hot and dry, is agreeably cool, but in an atmosphere rendered oppressive and unpleasant by the want of a free circulation of air, and the smell and smoke of gunpowder.

The works are being carried on each way from this shaft and whichever way you go the same appearance meets you. The dark dim vault, filled with clouds of vapour, is saved from utter blackness by the feeble light of candles which are stuck upon the sides of the excavation, and placed on trucks or other things used in carrying on the works; these which in your immediate neighbourhood emit a dull red light, are seen gradually diminishing in size and effect, till they appear like small red dots, and are then lost in the dark void.

Taking a candle in your hand you pick your way through the pools of water, over the temporary rails, among blocks of stone and the huge chains attached to the machinery which every now and then impede your way, happy and lucky if no impediment, unobserved in the dull uncertain light, should arrest your progress by causing you to measure your length on the wet and rugged floor.

Presently your attention is excited by a strange light before you, the perfect darkness above is broken by a faint, grey streak, which, at first scarcely perceptible, soon assumes a stronger hue; you protest till you find yourself and your companions standing under an opening from above in an uncertain and unearthly light, looking like ghosts just returning from a visit to the abode of man and hastening to their dark and dreary homes. This opening is an air shaft, and is made to ventilate the tunnel.

Pursuing your onward course, examining by the way the appearance of the works, and admiring the solid walls which nature has provided, you note every now and then a beautiful rill, clear as crystal, issuing from some fissure in the rock, trickling down the sides of the tunnel, and helping to form one of the many pools and streams with which the floor yet abounds. Nor during this time have your ears been idle, the sounds of the pick, the shovel and the hammer, have fallen upon them indistinctly; but as you advance they increase, and the hum of distant voices is heard. The faint illumination, before only just sufficient to make darkness visible, now becomes stronger, and the lights which have been placed chiefly in line along the walls become more frequent, they dot the whole of the opening being pretty thickly planted from the floor to the roof.

The cause for this is soon apparent, as you advance a busy scene opens before you, gangs of men are at work on all sides, and the tunnel, which to this point had been cut to its full dimensions, suddenly contracts; you leave the level of the floor, and scrambling up among the workmen, stepping sometimes on the solid rock, at others on loose fragments, you wind your way slowly and with difficulty.

Having been informed that a shot is about to be fired at the further extremity, you stop to listen and to judge its effect. The match is applied, the explosion follows, and a concussion such as probably you never felt before, takes place, the solid rock appears to shake, and the reverberation of the sound and shock is sensibly and fearfully experienced; another and another to follow, and with a slight stretch of the imagination you might fancy yourself in the midst of a thundercloud with heaven's artillery booming around.

You pursue your rugged path and having arrived at the part where the junction was made between the two cuttings, you have the opportunity of examining the roof, and of admiring the solid bed of rock of which it is formed, and of appreciating the skill which enabled the engineer to keep true course under all the difficulties of such a work.

After traversing a considerable space within reach of the roof, you find your way to the bottom, among a gang of labourers who are working from the other end, and having arrived at the shaft at the Chippenham side of the tunnel, you step upon the platform, the word is given, and you are once more elevated to the surface of the earth, glad to breathe the pure air, and full of wonder at the skill, enterprise, and industry of your fellow men.

An advertisement for auction of contractor's plant used for constructing Box Tunnel, 6 July 1841. (Bath & Cheltenham Gazette)

The former Tunnel Inn, Box Hill, 4 April 2002, used by railway navvies.

(C.G. Maggs)

The *Wiltshire Independent* of 11 July 1839 reported, regarding the union between Lewis and Brewer's tunnel workings:

> But, on breaking through the last intervening portion of rock, the accuracy of the headings was proved, and to the joy of the workmen, who took a lively interest in the result and to the triumph of Messrs Lewis and Brewer's scientific working, it was found that the junction was perfect to A HAIR AS TO THE LEVEL, the entire roof forming an unvarying line; while laterally, the utmost deviation from a straight line was only ONE INCH AND A QUARTER!

This was a great achievement for 1,520 ft begun at opposite ends. Brunel was so delighted that he took a ring from his finger and presented it to the ganger beside him.

The *Bath Chronicle* of 5 March 1840 commented that an increase of water in the tunnel had impeded progress; that three additional shafts had been sunk and from two of them the excavation of the tunnel had commenced, thus raising the general rate of progress. About 1,900 yd or two-thirds of the tunnel had been excavated and 580 yd of this had been carried out in the last six months, leaving 1,220 yd to be completed. On 15 July 1840 the sides of No. 5A shaft fell, killing two men and seriously injuring five. At the end of February 1841 less than 50 yd of the tunnel remained to be excavated and completion was anticipated in four to six weeks. The tunnel was to be extended a few yards at its eastern end to reduce the amount of excavation in the approach cutting. On 14 April 1841 the last length of excavation by Burge was finished. A letter of 22 June 1841 to Thomas Osler, Bristol, secretary of the GWR, from William Glennie, resident engineer of the tunnel, requested that no more visitors be admitted to view the tunnel.

To reassure passengers that the tunnel was perfectly safe, its portals had a particularly solid appearance, that at the west end being especially attractive and certainly enhancing its surroundings. The formers used for constructing the mouth were recycled by Burge and used for a building at Herne Bay. To cater for double track, the tunnel had a width of 30 ft at the springing of the arch, while the soffit was 25 ft above rail level.

Building Box Tunnel involved considerable risk to life and limb, although the hundred deaths mentioned in some accounts is probably exaggerated, as between September 1839 and November 1840, the period during which almost half the tunnel was excavated, the GWR reported ten deaths, while local papers recorded only a handful of fatalities.

On 10 May 1838 a fatal accident occurred when a man slipped and fell 60 ft down a shaft, and on 30 June 1838 a workman had come by lift to the top of shaft No. 5 to take refreshment when his foot slipped and he fell 260 ft. On 4 August 1838 an inquest was held at Box Tunnel Inn on Charles Day, aged twenty, a bricklayer's labourer who on the previous day was on a swinging scaffold repairing brickwork about 50 ft above the bottom of Shaft No. 3 when a descending empty skip struck and tilted the scaffolding. Day fell to the bottom, but the other two workmen clung to ropes until the scaffold righted itself. On 21 February 1839 Charles Higgins, aged twenty-one, was fatally injured when blasting, and five days later Charles Griffin, a miner at No. 5 shaft, was passing under bricklayers' scaffolding when it fell and killed him. On 17 November 1839, when wheeling his barrow over a plank across a shaft, a workman missed his footing and fell to his death. Eight days later, at No. 2 shaft, David Lee, subcontractor of the shaft, descended to inspect the work and was fatally injured by falling timbers. As seven men were working at No. 5 shaft on 15 July 1840 its sides fell in, killing one man outright, while another died later and two more were 'not expected to recover'. The other three were 'very much injured'. Eight days later Sheppard, a young man from Atworth, in a state of intoxication entered the engine house at No. 7 shaft and while asleep rolled under the sway beam 'which came down violently on his head and smashed it to pieces'.

Chapter Two

OPENING THE LINE

FARINGDON ROAD TO WOOTTON BASSETT ROAD

Works on the Faringdon Road to Wotton Bassett Road were finished in December 1840 and Lt Col. Sir Frederic Smith made the Board of Trade inspection. Of the temporary terminus at Wootton Bassett Road (or Hay Lane), nearly 4 miles from the town, he wrote: 'Although Hay Lane Station is merely intended as a temporary terminus, the Company are forming it, in regard to sidings, switches and other mechanical arrangements, in the same extensive and substantial manner as is their ordinary practice at permanent terminals.' As some expected the line to be opened on 15 December, the railway had post horses placed at Wootton Bassett Road so that any arriving passengers could be taken to Faringdon Road (renamed Challow on 1 June 1864) without delay. On 16 December 1840 'A vast concourse of persons assembled on Wootton Bassett Road station to see the extending of this line of railway' (*Bath Chronicle*), but were disappointed because the Board of Trade's inspection required a slight modification. Contrasting with the bustle of the previous day, the extension through Swindon to Wootton Bassett Road station opened quietly on 17 December, the first train leaving for Paddington at 10.15 a.m. for Wootton Bassett Road. The inhabitants of Swindon who wished to travel by rail had to catch their train at Wootton Bassett Road, as the junction station was still incomplete. The GWR arranged with the proprietors of the Bristol and Bath coaches to offer a fixed mileage rate between Wootton Bassett Road and Bath (the Bristol to Bath section of the GWR had opened on 31 August 1840), carrying passengers and parcels booked through by the GWR. Similar arrangements were made for goods traffic. Although from the map it would seem beneficial to have used Wootton Basset Road as the railhead for Gloucester traffic, because the roads in the Wootton Bassett district were so appalling, Gloucester traffic continued to use Faringdon Road.

WOOTTON BASSETT ROAD TO CHIPPENHAM

On 11 May 1841 the *Bath & Cheltenham Gazette* reported that works from Wootton Bassett Road to Chippenham would be opened on 1 June 1841 (actually it was 31 May 1841), that nearly all the permanent way was laid and,

> The works in the neighbourhood of Wootton Bassett have been proceeding with extraordinary rapidity lately; and there have been several accidents during the past week. One man had four ribs broken from a piece of wood falling on him; and another had his leg so badly fractured that immediate amputation was deemed necessary. They were both well taken care of by the contractor, and are both doing well.

Sir Frederic Smith inspected the 13¾ miles of line from Wootton Bassett Road to Chippenham in mid-May 1841 and found it insufficiently complete for public traffic. At a second inspection towards the end of the month Smith wrote:

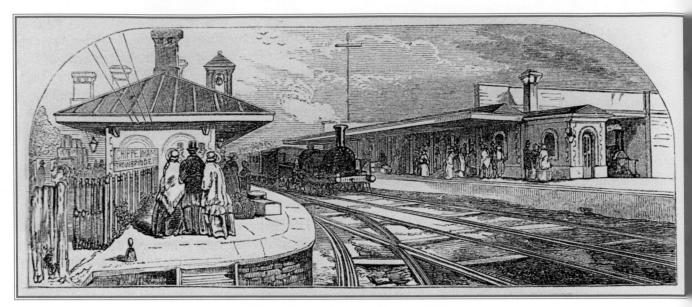

Chippenham station, view Down, *c.* 1853.

(G. Measom)

In that portion of the Line which extends from Hay Lane to Chippenham there are four deep cuttings; the first of the extreme depth of 40 feet; the second of nearly 50 feet, the third of 40 feet and the fourth of 50 feet.

There are 3 embankments of the respective extreme heights of 40 feet, of 30 feet and of 33 feet; and another embankment of the total length of 3¾ miles and of an extreme depth of about 20 feet.

Owing to the unfavorable [*sic*] season of the year at which the first two lofty embankments were formed, and owing also to their being composed chiefly of clay they have slipped to such an extent as to render it necessary to endeavour to secure them by several rows of piles driven through the mass into the natural ground. The performance of this work delayed the opening of the line for some weeks.

Considerable subsidence may still be expected, but I trust no danger will arise from this circumstance as the Superintendent of the Line, alive to the risk to which passengers would be exposed by any want of vigilance, will I doubt not adopt proper precautions especially in the approaching winter for the safety of the Travellers.

The remainder of the embankments and the cuttings are in good order and the permanent way of a very satisfactory description.

The fences with few exceptions are complete, and the bridges generally of larger dimensions and more convenient than required by the Acts of Parliament.

The gates for the several crossings were to be put up on the day appointed for the opening and the mile posts were on the ground on the day of my Inspection.

The station at Chippenham will afford ample accommodation to the public but it is not quite complete. The temporary station at Hay Lane is to be abandoned as soon as the station house and other buildings which are now forming at Swindon shall be completed.

The establishment proposed to be added for the portion of line between Hay Lane and Chippenham appears to be sufficient.

The system of signals on this Railway seems well calculated for the safety of the public. The principle adopted is as follows:

There is placed on a lofty pole, a horizontal board, which on being turned full on the line shows a black bar. When this signal is exhibited no train or engine is allowed to approach the station. On the same pole, but on a higher level a round disk is placed. This disk presents its edge up and down the line when the cross bar is exhibited and these signals denote that the station must not be entered, but when the disk is visible up and down the line, and the cross bar turned so as to present its edge, then it is understood that the station is open for any engine or train. Thus the engine drivers have both a negative and positive signal for their guidance the exhibition of the cross bar and the non exhibition of the disk signifying that they are not to approach and on the other hand when the disk is visible and the cross bar is not seen, the station is considered to be clear.

As these signals differ so essentially from those in use upon other lines, and appear so well calculated for the object in view I have thought it right to bring them under your special notice.

At each station there are also two flags. The red one is used to denote that another engine or train is not more than 3 minutes a head [*sic*]; and the green flag is intended to signify that another engine or train has passed within 10 minutes.

The night signals are upon the same principles as those in use by day.

With reference to this railway I have only to add, that I am not aware that the Acts of Parliament have been deviated from in any essential points, or in any manner prejudicial to the public.

On the arrival at Chippenham of the first train from Paddington on 31 May 1841 the chairman and several directors, Brunel and officers of the company were entertained at a public breakfast by the mayor and leading citizens. Chippenham station was still not quite complete.

The *Bath & Cheltenham Gazette* of 1 June 1841 reported: 'The day was exceedingly fine and we are informed that the various trains throughout the day were much crowded, and formed great objects of curiosity to the inhabitants of the vicinage.'

GREAT WESTERN RAILWAY.
Large SALE of RAILWAY PLANT,
On Contracts Nos. 5 and 6, near WOOTTON BASSETT, Wilts.

MR. C. HUNT begs to announce that this extensive SALE (previously Advertised) will take place on MONDAY, the 16th August next, and following Days.

The Plant comprises a great variety, such as Waggons, Sleepers, Wheeling-planks, Wheelbarrows, Bridge-centreings, Leggings, Battens, Bars (of different descriptions), Chairs, Crossings, Blacksmiths' Shop, Office, and Building, Blacksmiths' Tools, quantity of odd Timber, Pug-mills, Timber-carriage, &c. &c. &c.

N.B. Catalogues to be obtained of the Auctioneer, Wootton Bassett, a few days prior to the Sale, which will commence each day at Eleven o'Clock. In consequence of the great number of Lots, the favour of an early attendance is requested.

The First Day's Sale will take place in Friday Street, Christian Malford.

Wootton Bassett, July 21st, 1841.   1053

An advertisement for auction of railway plant at Christian Malford, 16 August 1841.
(Bath & Cheltenham Gazette)

Wootton Bassett incline, 1846. To the left are a policeman's hut and a capstan for turning the points.
(Engraving by J.C. Bourne)

The Revd Charles Young took his parish clerk, William Hinton, to see one of the first trains descend Dauntsey Bank. Young wrote:

The novelty of the sight, the strangeness of the sounds, the marvellous velocity with which engine, tender, carriages and trucks disappeared, the dense columns of sulphurous smoke, were altogether too much for the reason of my simple dominie [Hinton], and he fell prostrate on the bank-side as if he had been smitten by a thunderbolt! When he had recovered his feet, his brain still reeled, his tongue clove to the roof of his mouth, and he stood aghast, unutterable amazement stamped upon his face. It must have been quite five minutes before he could speak, and when he did it was in the tone of a Jeremiah. 'Well, Sir, that was a sight to have seen; but one I never care to see again! How much longer shall knowledge be allowed to go on increasing?'

The opening to Chippenham brought Bath within about five hours of London. Coaches which hitherto had made one journey a day between the railheads, were now able to make two, and one even three. There was a shortage of coachmen – presumably realising that their jobs were under threat, they had found other employment – so those normally working just within Bath drove to Chippenham.

The opening seriously affected places not on the route of the railway. Before the line opened, thirty to forty coaches a day ran through Marlborough, but the advent of the GWR reduced this number to five. The £2,000 paid annually to horse keepers and helpers and then spent within Marlborough was no longer received. From the spring of 1840 only one Bath coach (it ran from the Castle and Ball Inn) proceeded all the way by road from Bath to London without using the railway. The *Bath & Cheltenham Gazette* of 28 April 1840 recorded that innkeepers between Bath and Reading were 'starving' and that the value of tavern property within that area had been reduced within the last two to three years by 60 to 80 per cent.

On 6 July 1841 a letter in the *Bath & Cheltenham Gazette* observed that the first-class fare from Wootton Bassett to Chippenham was 4*s* 6*d* for 13 miles, whereas the 12 miles from Bath to Bristol and 14 miles from Maidenhead to Reading had a first-class fare of only 2*s* 6*d*.

Meanwhile, west of Box Tunnel, deviations from the original plan delayed purchase of land until 1839. The contractor started that summer. Delays were caused by the diversion of the turnpike road west of Box station and the contractor's failure in 1840. In February 1841 Brunel reported that Middle Hill Tunnel was almost finished, but that the bridge at Bathford was in arrears and difficulties had been experienced diverting the Kennet & Avon Canal at Hampton Row. The GWR was required to pay the canal company £7,660 for stopping boats while the diversion was being carried out. The *Bath & Cheltenham Gazette* of 13 April 1841 said, 'On Tuesday morning (5 April) the channel of the new cut to divert water of the canal near Hampton Row, Bath, in order to afford space for the railroad adjoining, was finally completed, and the water let in.'

The edition for 29 June quotes from the *Bristol Journal*:

This unrivalled line now on the eve of completion, will be opened throughout on Wednesday next. London will thus be brought within four hours' distance (if the term may be used) of Bristol and by the continuation is within 5½ hours of Bridgwater. The fares are very moderate, and passengers have no vexatious fees to pay in addition. Travelling on this line is a perfect luxury, not merely on account of the speed obtained by the broad gauge and machinery of the first class, but by the feeling that perfect safety is ensured (as far as human effort can vail) by the admirable construction of the works; which also is enhanced by the enjoyment of ease and comfort, arising from the equable motion of the carriages, such as can be experienced on no other line.

The *Bath & Cheltenham Gazette* agreed with these sentiments and its issue of 27 July commented: 'It is now admitted that in every point of view the Great Western is the best, whether for speed, safety, or absence of unpleasant motion.'

CHIPPENHAM TO BATH

Brunel had intended opening the 26¾ miles from Wootton Bassett Road to Bath in early June 1841, but despite bonuses to contractors and workmen, and work continuing twenty-four hours a day, the section from Chippenham to Bath was incomplete. Sir Frederic Smith made an inspection and reported to the GWR secretary, Charles Saunders:

Bath June 28th 1841

Sir,

With references to your notice of it being the intention of the Directors of the Great Western Railway Company to open on the 30th Instant, that portion of their line which will connect Chippenham with Bath, and thus complete that magnificent work which will afford railway communication between the Metropolis and Bristol; I have to acquaint you that I have inspected the portion of the line in question, and which I desire to express my unqualified praise of the finished parts of the railway it is necessary that I should point out to you those works which will require to be put into a more complete state before the contemplated opening. These consist chiefly of Fences, Ballasting and Bridges.

In the first place, there are, in various parts of the line, gaps in the fences, which for the safety of the public, it is indispensable to fill up; though in some spots of small extent, these deficiencies notwithstanding demand attention, and I am particularly desirous of bringing your notice the Fences at the following places viz.

Between the 94th and 95 mile posts.

Near the Patterdown Bridge.

The approach to Chapman's Bridge, where the fences are insecurely fixed.

At Thingley Bridge where the line is not fenced in from the road.

Between the Bath Road Bridge and the Avon, where the railway is contiguous to the Turnpike road, a fence is required to separate them.

Near Rose Mount Cottage a considerable length of Fence is required.

The foregoing are all essential to prevent cattle straying upon the line thereby endangering the safety of the traveller, and it would if practicable, be desirable that, before the opening the parapet wall along the top of the retaining wall, between the canal and the railway, as well as the balustrade to separate the railway from Sydney Gardens should be built.

With respect to the Bridges I have the following observations to make:

The south-western wing wall of the first Bridge beyond the Chippenham Station is slightly bulged. As the embankment which this wall retains is lofty, and serious mischief might result from its giving way at the moment a train might be passing, it is very desirable that steps should be taken at the first convenient opportunity to remedy this defect.

At a short distance from this bridge there is an occupation passage through the embankment. The flank walls are unfinished, and the arch is supported by timbers to resist the weight pressing against it. These points require early attention.

The coping is unfinished of the Bridge over the London Turnpike road.

The side walls of Patterdown Bridge are crippled; if there be room between them they had better be strengthened by external piers, and if not, it may be necessary that the walls should be taken down and rebuilt.

Chapman's Bridge will require to be early underpinned, as well as the northern pier of Pound Hill Bridge, and the parapet wall of the latter should be forthwith built.

The Aqueduct between Pound Hill Bridge and Potley Lane Bridge, is I presume not yet finished, nor is the parapet of the latter.

The Balustrade and wing walls of the entrance of the Box Tunnel are still incomplete, as is the coping of the Ashly [sic] Green Bridge.

The Bridge for the parish road near Sydney Gardens; the approach to the adjacent Iron Bridge; and the coping and approach of the Bridge east of it, are unfinished. It is of great importance to the public safety that if these Bridges should not be finished before the opening of the line, the strictest orders should be issued to prevent any obstruction being thrown on the rails in the course of the operations for their completion.

The permanent way is yet far from finished, but as the embankments are complete, and the cuttings, with few exceptions, cleared out, it may be possible to lay the remainder of the rails by the 30th, but I am desirous of recommending that great attention may be paid to their being properly screwed down to the timbers, in which I at present observe a deficiency.

The ballasting is generally scanty and especially at some of the outer curves, on the lofty embankments. This point wants peculiar care.

I am glad to find that it is the intention to remove some earth which is still in one of the cuttings by means of an extra line, so as to avoid those chances of accident which would exist if for that purpose either of the permanent lines of rails were to be used.

The distance posts are not yet put up for the greater part of the line intended to be opened. It is indispensable that this deficiency should be supplied.

Although is the day which you proposed for my inspection, yet you will perceive from the foregoing account, and you must be aware from your personal knowledge of the state of the works, that they are not in such forwardness as to justify my unconditionally sanctioning the opening on the 30th Instant. I shall however with the hope of meeting the wishes of the Directors and the convenience of the public, so far as may be consistent with my duty, make another complete inspection of the works tomorrow; but as I even then do not reckon upon their being finished, I can only sanction the opening of this portion of the line with the clear understanding that your Chief Engineer satisfies himself, by a personal inspection, before the running of the first train, that all the points which I have mentioned have received that degree of attention which is essential to the public safety; and I earnestly hope that for a few days the rate of speed may be moderate over the newly laid portion of the line.

I need hardly add that I rely on your having fulfilled all the Stipulations of the Acts of Parliament bearing upon the portion of the line new under consideration, and that you will not fail to extend to it the same degree of care in the arrangements for the Police, Signals and other means of protecting the public from accidents that prevails on other parts of the Great Western Railway.

In conclusion I would call to your recollection that the signal posts have not yet been put up.

I have etc.

Frederic Smith
Lt Colonel R Engineers
Inspector General of Railways

In reply to this, Charles Saunders, the GWR secretary, and Daniel Gooch, the locomotive superintendent, undertook personally to superintend traffic until everything had been fully completed. At 3 a.m. on 30 June Brunel and Sir Frederic Smith went over the line from Chippenham to Bath on an engine and tender, returning at 8 a.m. Smith agreed to the line being opened subject to safety being guaranteed.

The west portal of Box Tunnel, 1846.

(Engraving by J.C. Bourne)

The line opened to the public on 30 June 1841, the only mishap that day being a Down train which derailed approaching Bath station. After an hour it was re-railed and took the train on to Bristol. As only a single line was complete through Box Tunnel, for the first forty-eight hours Gooch personally acted as pilotman to every train. On the second night, while on the footplate of the last Up train, he saw a green light ahead. (At that period locomotives carried green headlights and passenger coaches displayed a green lamp forward.) Realising that the Down Mail was on the same road, he quickly reversed back to Box station. The policeman at the Corsham end had failed to hold the train and, had the tunnel not been free of steam and smoke, a head-on collision would have occurred. When Gooch did eventually take the Up train through it became derailed, and he spent all night getting it back on the road. He wrote in his diary:

> I need not say I was not sorry to get home and to be at Paddington after two days and nights' pretty hard work. Mr Brunel was at the time living in Bath, and he was very kind to me in sending me plenty of good food, &c, to keep my steam up. Box tunnel had a very pretty effect for a couple of days it was worked as a single line, from the number of candles used by the men working on the unfinished line; it was a perfect illumination, extending through the whole tunnel.

The *Bath Chronicle* made no mention of the opening from Chippenham to the city, deeming election news more important. There was no public ceremony at the opening, but a beflagged train carrying the directors left Paddington at 8 a.m., arriving at Bristol at noon and Bridgwater at 1.30 p.m. The first train between Bath and Chippenham for public use left Temple Meads at 7 a.m. for Paddington. On that day about 100 flags decorated the western portal of Box Tunnel and the adjacent road bridge, while a band played and George Burge's foreman, on behalf of the contractor, distributed 3 hogsheads of beer, or about 1,200 pints. In the evening an entertainment for those concerned with management was held at the Queen's Head, Box.

The first engine to attempt the climb through the tunnel was 'Sun' class 2–2–2 *Meridian*, driven by Cuthbert Davison with an anxious Brunel beside him on the footplate. Unlike Brunel, Gooch had no worries about locomotives being unable to work the 1 in 100 through Box Tunnel. Gooch commented: 'I cannot say I felt any anxiety, as I had seen how well our engines took their load up Wootton Bassett without the help of a bank-engine, and with the assistance of a bank-engine at Box, I felt we would have no difficulty.'

In its issue of 20 July 1841 the *Bath & Cheltenham Gazette* described a journey through Box Tunnel:

> You have passed the gloomy portal, and now you begin to experience a set of feelings to which you have hitherto been a stranger. You feel an undefined feeling of awe, but yet that feeling partakes more of sublimity than of terror. You thunder on, the atmosphere every moment growing more tenebrous than before, till presently you are involved in utter darkness. It is now you are fairly in the tunnel; hurried at a fearful rate through the bowels of the everlasting hills. It is now, if possible, darker than ever. The air is chill and sepulchral. You are no longer a passenger in a railway. You have left the earth and all its concerns far behind, and are now being hurried through the regions of perpetual night by the fiery demon who cleaves the murky air with a speed belonging to nought but a creature of darkness! Hark how he screams with savage delight, as though in the very wantonness of fiendish exultation; and how the cry is taken up and re-echoed through the gloomy cavern. To cry – to shriek for help – is useless. Those who

A train climbing the gradient of 1 in 100 through Box Tunnel, 1846.
The policeman on the right shines his lantern to signify 'All Clear'.

(Engraving by J.C. Bourne)

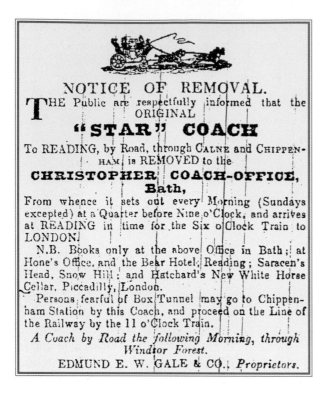

NOTICE OF REMOVAL.

THE Public are respectfully informed that the
ORIGINAL

"STAR" COACH

To READING, by Road, through CALNE and CHIPPEN-
HAM is REMOVED to the

CHRISTOPHER COACH-OFFICE,
Bath,

From whence it sets out every Morning (Sundays
excepted) at a Quarter before Nine o'Clock, and arrives
at READING in time for the Six o'Clock Train to
LONDON.
  N.B. Books only at the above Office in Bath; at
Hone's Office, and the Bear Hotel, Reading; Saracen's
Head, Snow Hill; and Hatchard's New White Horse
Cellar, Piccadilly, London.
  Persons fearful of Box Tunnel may go to Chippen-
ham Station by this Coach, and proceed on the Line of
the Railway by the 11 o'Clock Train.
  A Coach by Road the following Morning, through
Windsor Forest.
  EDMUND E. W. GALE & CO., *Proprietors.*

An advertisement for travel by
the 'Star' coach, 27 July 1841.
(Bath & Cheltenham Gazette)

could help are far behind; and you are every moment plunging deeper into those fearful
regions. See how the baleful gleams from the eyes of the monster light the damp sides of his
chill abode. Suddenly a ray of light shoots through the gloom. You look up: there – far, far up
– appears the deep blue of the summer sky you are doomed never again to behold. One
moment – (one single glance is all you can catch of it) – it is gone, and the darkness is tenfold
darker than before! How the monster rushes on! How his cavern reverberates in thunder to his
mighty progress! . . . But what gleams in the distance? – surely some star that has lost its way,
and wandered into these regions of darkness. But yet it cannot be: each moment it increases in
size. It is – it is – the sign of returning day. Look! there is the blue sky, there is the green turf
once more; . . . and the exit of Box Tunnel appears in our rear, still vomiting forth from its
tremendous jaws the steam which we have left behind in our passage.

The opinion was widely held, even by some doctors, that no passenger could possibly
survive two journeys through the tunnel, and a good many people took what was
considered a wise precaution of leaving the train at the station before the tunnel,
covering the distance between the two stations by road and joining a train again when
there was no longer any risk in doing so of exposure to the dangerous atmosphere of the
tunnel. *Keene's Bath Journal* for 26 July 1841 contained a public notice regarding the 'Star'
coach: 'Persons fearful of Box Tunnel may go to Chippenham by this coach, and proceed
on the line of railway by the 11 o'clock train.' For the benefit of those who wished to
avoid the tunnel, the Railway Hotel with about eighteen rooms was established at
Corsham, but apart from the very early days, its size proved a white elephant.

In an attempt to overcome tunnel phobia the directors proposed lighting be installed,
but Brunel asked them to abandon the idea as the tunnel was no darker than the rest of
the line at night and lighting would be 'very costly'. The *Bath & Cheltenham Gazette* of

6 July 1841 found no problem: 'The three great *desiderata* of a tunnel, viz absence from danger, darkness and damp, have been perfectly overcome. It is now so dry that one might walk through it in slippers. It is lighted by six shafts which by day give sufficient light, and is as safe as any other part of the line.'

The early fear of Box Tunnel was still a reality on 18 May 1870, when the Revd Robert Kilvert entered in his diary:

In Box Tunnel, as there was no lamp, people began to strike foul brimstone matches and hand them to each other all down the carriage. All the time we were in the tunnel these lighted matches were travelling from hand to hand in the darkness. Each match lasted the length of the carriage and the red ember was thrown out of the opposite window, by which time another match was seen travelling down the carriage. The carriage was chock full of fumes . . . and by the time we got out of the tunnel I was almost suffocated.

Early in August 1841 the inhabitants met in Corsham Town Hall and requested that the GWR provide a goods station, as the expense of cartage from Chippenham to Corsham was almost as much as the carriage paid from Bristol, and therefore many people in Corsham continued to have goods sent by road. On 31 August the *Bath & Cheltenham Gazette* reported that it was claimed that almost 200 tons of goods had been carried to and from Corsham by canal and road wagons in the two months that the GWR had been open, in consequence of the company not yet having made a goods station. The same month Corsham passenger station was used by 'throngs of visitors' to see Lord Methuen's superb collection of paintings which could be seen daily, instead of just Mondays when the family was at home.

A Trowbridge correspondent to the *Bath & Cheltenham Gazette* of 24 August 1841 extolled the virtues of the GWR. He said that in 1807 he left Ludgate Hill, London, at 1 p.m. and did not arrive at Trowbridge until 9.30 a.m. the next day. In July 1841 a basket of plums was sent to London by GWR, not leaving Trowbridge until 10 a.m. and by 5 p.m. that same afternoon those plums were in an oven 2 miles from Paddington station and the pie eaten the same evening!

The dangers of the new line were not always readily apparent. On 31 August 1841 a labourer on the GWR just south of Chippenham crossed over to the Up line in order to avoid an approaching Down train and failed to see an Up train approaching. It whistled, but the noise of the Down train drowned the sound. He was killed. The *Bath & Cheltenham Gazette* commented unsympathetically: 'When the carelessness of the workmen, and the very short time they allow themselves to get out of the way, are taken into consideration, it will not be wondered at that accidents should occasionally occur.'

Chapter Three

DESCRIPTION OF THE LINE

Swindon Junction station has a particularly interesting history. It was established at the junction of the GWR and Cheltenham & Great Western Union Railway and, because of the establishment of the railway factory, became important in its own right. As the cost of building the GWR had exceeded the estimated expenditure, the directors believed they had struck a bargain when they signed a contract with Messrs J. & C. Rigby for that firm to construct the station for nothing and lease it to the GWR for a penny a year, the GWR undertaking to stop all passenger trains at Swindon for 10 minutes. The idea was that Messrs Rigby would recoup their costs from catering profits.

The station, 307 ft above sea level, opened on 14 July 1842, nineteen months after the opening of the line through Swindon to Wootton Bassett Road. Designed by Brunel, it consisted of two island platforms, on each of which was a three-storey stone building of 170 ft × 37 ft. Kitchens and offices were set in the basements; at platform level were the first-class and second-class refreshment rooms – no such facilities were provided for third class – and the upper floors formed a hotel. The twin buildings were linked by a covered footbridge used by passengers and hotel guests until a subway was built in 1870, after which it was used only by the hotel. The walls and ceilings of the refreshment rooms were elaborately decorated. George Measom's *Official Illustrated Guide to the Great Western Railway*, published in 1852, enthused:

> A glance down yonder staircase leading to the kitchens below us, amply fitted with culinary apparatus, pantries and store-rooms filled to repletion with every solid article of food that reasonable man can wish for and spacious cellars, whose bins are full of the choicest wines, and whose shelves groan under the weight of hundreds of dozens of porter, ale, soda water etc. . . . Ascend to the upper floor: there you will find a noble coffee-room, private sitting rooms, etc. (with bedrooms on the other side of the line), in fact, nearly all the appurtenances of a first-rate family hotel, nearly every window of which commands magnificent views of the Wiltshire and Berkshire scenery for many miles around.

The two inner platform roads were used by Bristol trains and the outer by those to and from Gloucester, the island design facilitating interchange. Each platform measured 184 ft × 68 ft. Swindon was the only important early GWR station not to have an overall roof.

Within a week of signing the lease Messrs Rigby had let the station to S.Y. Griffiths of Queen's Hotel, Cheltenham for seven years at a premium of £6,000 and an annual rent of £1,100. In August 1848 Rigby's sold the lease to J.R. Phillips for £20,000 and in April 1875 it was bought by G. Moss for £45,000. Following two more changes of ownership the GWR purchased the lease for £100,000 and abolished the frustrating 10 minute compulsory stop. On 1 October 1895 hundreds of works employees watched the 10.15 a.m. Paddington to Penzance and the 10.45 a.m. Paddington to South Wales pass through Swindon non-stop for the first time.

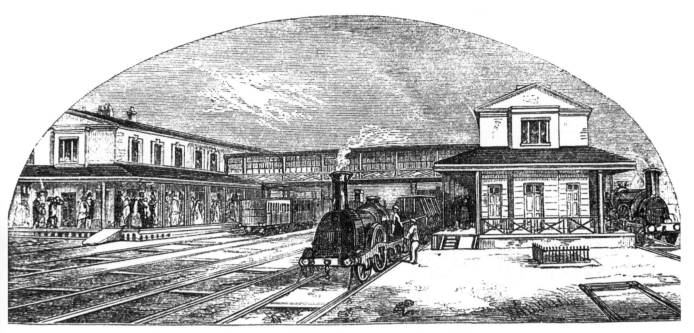

The eastern end of Swindon Junction station, *c.* 1853.

(*G. Measom*)

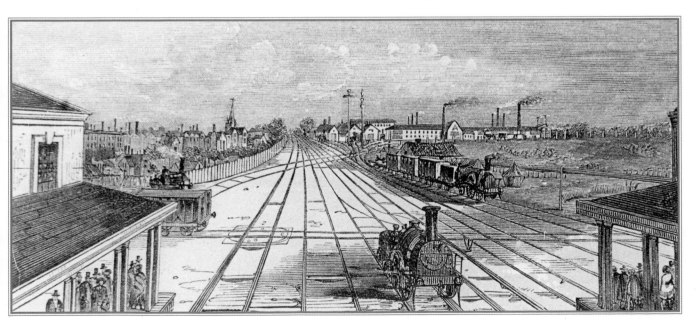

The view west from Swindon Junction station, *c.* 1853.
Notice the works in the right background and the wagon turntable to the centre left.

(*G. Measom*)

The first-class refreshment rooms, Swindon Junction, *c.* 1850.

(*G. Measom*)

However, this was not the end of the refreshment rooms, as at the end of the nineteenth century the rooms, known as the Queen's Royal Hotel, were famous for splendid catering, even the Prince of Wales (later King Edward VII) sometimes hiring a special train to take his friends there to dine.

Before the abolition of the compulsory stop the GWR was not always punctilious in the time spent at Swindon and sometimes trains left after a call of only 7 minutes. F.S. Williams wrote in *Our Iron Roads*:

On 7 August 1891 a Mr Lowenfield joined the 3.00 p.m. train at Paddington, with a first class ticket to Teignmouth. The time of the arrival of the train at Swindon was 4.27, and it was booked to leave again, of course, at 4.37. Since he was not due to reach Teignmouth till 7.42, Mr Lowenfield, somewhat rashly perhaps, elected to take an early dinner during the Swindon stop. It may be that he demolished the peculiar fare, which Swindon dignified with the name of dinner, in eight minutes. If so, the Great Western was too fast for him, for the train only waited seven minutes, and when a presumably replete Mr Lowenfield stepped on to the platform it had gone.

Mr Lowenfield, of course, was furious. There was no further connection to Teignmouth for another four hours, and even on an August evening, there are perhaps few who would enjoy Swindon for that length of time. He accordingly decided to take the next train to Bristol, and ordered by telegraph a special train to be ready to convey him thence to Teignmouth.

Lowenfield's special may well have been the last to run over the broad gauge. It cost him £37 17*s*, which he paid with a cheque that the next morning he asked his bank to stop.

THE QUEEN'S ROYAL HOTEL

AND

REFRESHMENT BUFFETS,

(Swindon Junction Station, Great Western Railway.)

SPECIAL FEATURES.

1. The property is held on lease for 99 years (of which 56 years are unexpired) direct from the Great Western Railway Company, at a rental of one penny per annum, and is consequently very valuable. (See Messrs Daniel Cronin and Son's Report and Valuation on next page.)

2. By a covenant in the lease, all trains passing through Swindon Junction are compelled to stop for refreshments, and the Company, therefore, possesses a monopoly.

3. The business has been established and carried on with the greatest success for over 43 years.

4. The average net profits (as certified by Messrs. Quilter, Ball and Co.) amount to £7,237 7s. 2d. per annum, and are steadily increasing year by year.

The Railway, Tramway & General Trust, Limited,

OFFER FOR SALE

2,000 SHARES OF £5 EACH,

(Being part of a total Share Capital of £50,000, fully subscribed and allotted,) of

THE SWINDON JUNCTION HOTEL COMPANY,

LIMITED.

(Incorporated under the Companies' Acts, 1862 to 1883, whereby the liability of each Shareholder is limited to the amount (if any) unpaid on his Shares.)

The price required is £5 5s. per Share, payable as follows:—

10/- per Share on Application.
£2 5/- „ on Allotment.
£2 10/- the 15th March, 1886.

£5 5/-

The following Prospectus was issued by the Swindon Junction Hotel Company, Limited, when the Share Capital was offered for subscription and fully applied for.

Prospectuses and Forms of Application may be obtained of Messrs Brown, Janson & Co., 32, Abchurch Lane, London, E.C., or of the Railway, Tramway and General Trust, Limited, 28, Martin's Lane, Cannon Street, London, E.C.

PROSPECTUS.

THIS Company has been formed to purchase as a going concern and carry on the well-known "Queen's Royal Hotel," (so named on account of Her Majesty having stayed there when travelling), together with the Refreshment Rooms, &c., on the Up and Down Platforms at Swindon Junction Station of the Great Western Railway, which have been established and worked with the greatest success for over 43 years.

The property is held on lease direct from the Great Western Railway Company for 99 years (of which 56 years are unexpired) at a nominal rental of one penny per annum, and by a special covenant, all trains passing through Swindon Junction Station are compelled to stay there for refreshments for ten minutes. By a recent mutual agreement four Express Trains are allowed to stay for five minutes only.

The Lease was originally granted on these exceptional terms in consideration of a large premium paid to the Railway Company, and also the erection of all these buildings by the lessees; the trade having now developed to an enormous extent, the property has become exceedingly valuable.

The premises, which are fully licensed, consist of two First-class and two Second-class Refreshment Rooms, Bars, and Waiting Rooms, (on the Up and Down Platforms), Coffee, Dining, Private Sitting and Bedrooms above (the two blocks being connected by a private bridge over the lines), excellent Cellars, Kitchens, &c., &c. There is also a Public House, where a very large trade is done, chiefly among the employés (numbering about 6,000) of the Great Western Railway Company, at their Swindon Junction Works: in addition to which there are, excellent Stabling, Six Horses, Coach Houses, Yard, &c., and about two acres of ground, (with frontages to two main roads) suitable for the erection of from 15 to 20 cottages.

With a view to ascertaining the value of the premises, the Directors have instructed the eminent Hotel Valuers, Messrs Daniel Cronin and Sons, of 1, Vernon Place, Bloomsbury Square, W.C., to inspect the same, and their report, dated 28th January, 1886, states:—

"In accordance with your instructions, we have made a careful valuation of the Queen's Royal Hotel and Refreshment Rooms at Swindon Junction Station on the Great Western Railway. As we are instructed that the premises are held for an unexpired term of 56 years, direct from the Great Western Railway Company, at one penny per annum, we are of opinion that the premises are worth at least £70,000, and we are confirmed in our opinion by the fact that these premises were sold some years ago for a similar sum, and have greatly improved in value since."

The Trade being entirely Cash, there is absolutely no risk of bad debts, and as the Company possesses the exclusive right to sell refreshments at Swindon Junction Station (the Station on the Great Western Railway where all trains are compelled to stop for refreshments), competition is impossible.

The books have been examined by Messrs Quilter, Ball and Co., the well-known Chartered Accountants, and according to their report, the receipts from the 18th July, 1881, to 31st December, 1885, show an aggregate of £69,552 11s. 11d., the details of which are as follows:—

For the year ending 18th July, 1882,—£15,283 7s. 0d.
„ „ 18th July, 1883,—£15,103 5s. 4d.
„ „ 18th July, 1884,—£15,416 8s. 11d.
„ „ 18th July, 1885,—£15,955 5s. 3d.
From 19th July to 31st Dec., 1885,— £7,794 5s. 5d.

£69,552 11s. 11d.

Messrs Quilter, Ball and Co. have also taken out the profits from the 18th July, 1883, to 28th December, 1885 (a period of about 2 years and 5 months), and found them to be £17,677, viz.:—

For the year ending 18th July, 1884,—£6,757.
„ „ 1885,—£7,320.
From 19th July to 28th December, 1885,— £3,600.

£17,677.

An advertisement for shares in the Queen's Royal Hotel, Swindon Junction station.
(Stroud Journal, 6 March 1886)

The 10.30 a.m. Paddington–Plymouth express passes through Swindon Junction on 1 October 1895.
It was the first non-stop train after the GWR had purchased the refreshment rooms.

(Author's Collection)

The GWR brought an action against him for the cost of the special train. He responded with a counter-claim for damages, on the ground that the railway had failed to carry him to Teignmouth and had broken its contract by not stopping at Swindon for the stipulated 10 minutes. The judge agreed that Lowenfield was entitled to damages on account of the premature start, which he assessed at £2, and that he was also entitled to a refund of the first-class fare between Bristol and Teignmouth and to the reimbursement of the 3s spent on telegrams to an anxious family. The judge did not agree that the suffering which would have been caused to Lowenfield was such that he was justified in ordering a special. The GWR was therefore granted the recovery of the cost of the special and also the full costs of the action.

At about 2.30 a.m. on 26 March 1898, men in the yard noticed what they believed was a chimney fire in the Up station building. Every fireplace was examined and seemed in order when flames were spotted coming from the roof. Swindon Fire Brigade arrived at 3.50 a.m. and the GWR's own fire engine 10 minutes later. The conflagration was under control at 5.55 a.m. Charles Kislingbury, Divisional Superintendent, Bristol, received the news at his home in Montpelier, Bristol, just before 5 a.m. He left Temple Meads by special train at 6.15 a.m. and the locomotive and single coach arrived at Swindon at 7 a.m., giving an average speed of about 60 mph. What caused the fire? The chimney was Z-shaped and, although swept a fortnight before, its shape encouraged lodgement of soot, but more important was that a timber beam ran across the chimney, and matters were not aided by the fact that a lead gas pipe ran down the flue.

When inspecting the mixed gauge in November 1875 Col. Yolland commented that it was questionable in not keeping Gloucester traffic entirely on the north side of the station, because he believed that when the Severn Tunnel was opened and therefore more traffic came from Bristol, trains would be delayed by through Gloucester traffic starting from the south side of the station.

His advice was not taken and by 1929 the platforms were:

No. 1 – Down loop used by Gloucester trains
Nos 2 & 3 – Down bay platform roads
No. 4 – Down Main
No. 5 – Up Main
No. 6 – Up bay platform used by trains to the LNER
No. 7 – Up bay used for Highworth branch trains
No. 8 – Up loop used by trains from Gloucester

Following the withdrawal of local trains, the layout was rationalised and all traffic requiring the use of a platform was concentrated on the former Up island platform, the

Swindon Junction station after the fire, 26 March 1898.
Notice the exceptional length of the ladder in a period before extension ladders were common.

(Author's Collection)

Swindon Junction, view Down, *c.* 1890. Note the mixed-gauge track.

(Author's Collection)

The east end of Swindon Junction station, *c.* 1900. Notice the unusual lattice work from which
the main-line signals are suspended, and the horsebox standing at the Up main platform line.

(Author's Collection)

Swindon Junction Stationmaster Douse, left, with his staff, *c.* 1900.

(R. Brown)

new layout having the advantage that passengers changing trains no longer needed to change platforms. This layout was brought into use on 3 March 1968, coinciding with the introduction of a new signalling system for the area. One drawback with the new scheme was that Down trains requiring a platform had to cross the Up through road. To obviate this problem, Platform 4 on the Down side of the station opened on 2 June 2003 and resulted in immediate improvement in punctuality, particularly on routes to Bristol and South Wales which used the new platform.

On 9 May 1921 the staff employed at Swindon station consisted of:

Passenger staff: 5 booking clerks, 2 station clerks, 2 parcels clerks, 4 platform inspectors, 24 passenger guards, 15 shunters, 24 signalmen, 3 assistant signalmen, 6 telegraphists, 10 ticket collectors, 1 train ticket collector, 2 foremen passenger and goods, 2 leading parcels porters, 24 porters, 1 travelling parcels porter, 8 parcels porters, 2 signal lampmen, 4 station lampmen, 3 lamp lads, 2 cloakroom porters and 1 charwoman.

Goods staff: 7 yard inspectors, 55 goods guards, 39 shunters, 3 office porters and 2 lad porters.

Swindon station also had one of the most curious pieces of lost property. At the end of the nineteenth century an announcement appeared in the local paper that 'a pair of bright bay carriage horses, about 16 hands high, with black switch tails and manes' had been left by someone called Hibbert, and unless claimed and expenses paid they 'would be sold to pay expenses'. They were not claimed and were duly sold.

Aerial view of Swindon Junction station, with the carriage works to the left and wagon works to the right.

(Author's Collection)

Immediately west of Swindon station the Gloucester line curves northwards while that to Bristol passed the locomotive shops on the north side and carriage shops on the south. In 1919 the locomotive erecting shop was almost doubled in size to cover 11½ acres, making it the largest permanent workshop in Europe. Offices and toilets were situated in the roof to maximise floor space. In 1948 the whole works covered 326 acres, 77½ of which were roofed, but with the contraction of the railway system, by 1975 the works occupied only 147 acres, of which 34 were roofed. The works finally closed in June 1987.

Located 1¼ miles west of Swindon Junction station was Rushey Platt signal-box, where the Midland & South Western Junction Railway to Andover curved southwards, while the GWR main line passed under the MSWJR line to Cheltenham. Wootton Bassett Road station, near milepost 80, opened on 17 December 1840 and closed on 30 July 1841.

Shortly before Wootton Bassett station, the United Dairies siding trailed to the Up line at milepost 82¾; it was laid in 1927 and taken out of use in June 1972. During its construction 14,000 cubic yards of clay were excavated by J. Smith for £4,500, work starting mid-June and being complete by the end of September 1927. He used a steam navvy.

The dairy used the first rail bulk milk tanks to run in England, hitherto all such traffic had been in 17-gallon churns weighing 2¼ cwt when full. Tanks were more economical than churns. One man could rinse a tank with cold water and scrub it, gaining access through a manhole. It was then rinsed with hot water and finally sterilised with steam, a much easier operation than carrying out these procedures with the 176 17-gallon churns which held the equivalent of one tank. The 176 churns needed three vans to carry them and weighed a total of 80 tons, whereas one tank was only 22 tons. The 3,000-gallon

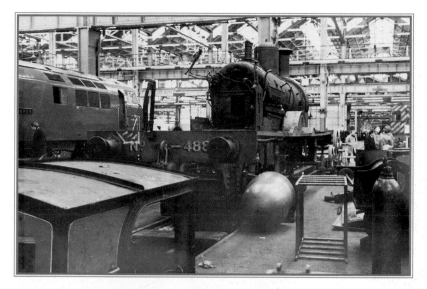

SR 4–4–2T No. 488,
now preserved on the
Bluebell Railway, and
diesel-hydraulic D1011
Western Thunderer
at Swindon Works,
November 1971.
*(R.J. Cannon, courtesy
C.G. Maggs)*

The locomotive
erecting shop, *c.* 1900.
(Author's Collection)

'A' wheel shop.
(Author's Collection)

GWR-built guns in 'AE' shop during the First World War.

(Author's Collection)

String used to check the alignment of the cylinder bore and horns on 4575 class 2–6–2T No. 5558.

(Author's Collection)

S160 class 2–8–0 No. 1604, built in the USA by ALCO during the Second World War, modified by the GWR and standing outside 'A' shop.

(Author's Collection)

Workers leaving the Rodbourne Road exit and delaying a Swindon Corporation double-decker electric tram.

(Author's Collection)

enamel glass-lined tanks were manufactured by the Dairy Supply Company, and the chassis was built at Swindon. Each tank was insulated with a 2 in layer of cork, which meant that the milk left the factory at 38°F and the temperature rose by no more than 1°F on its journey to Mitre Bridge siding, Willesden, the United Dairies' depot. The service was inaugurated on 1 December 1927, when a special train carrying 200 passengers was chartered to witness the filling of the tanks at Wootton Bassett.

On United Dairies' property were two loop sidings, each with a capacity of ten tank wagons. Outward traffic was placed on one siding and inward on the other. The tank wagons were moved by a cable attached to a lorry, the cable passing round a capstan. The gradient of the siding was 1 in 40 falling towards the main line. To prevent runaways fouling the main line, a spring point was provided between the loop and the boundary gate, and the man in charge of shunting operations held this closed when wagons were about to pass. The siding was worked by a locomotive sent light from Swindon at 1.30 p.m., leaving about an hour later with an average of fifteen milk tanks, the telegraph code of which was 'MILTA'. Later, the 1.05 p.m. Whitland to Paddington milk train picked up at the siding, obviating a special service. In 1954, classes of locomotive prohibited from using the siding were BR Standard classes 4, 5, 6, and 7, and all ex-GWR 4–6–0s.

The original station at Wootton Bassett was one of Brunel's chalet-style buildings erected in limestone. In readiness for the opening of the Bristol & South Wales Direct Railway, it was rebuilt in 1902 in red brick in the typical GWR architecture of the period by Eli Hadley & Sons at a cost of £4,409 16s 4d. Twelve months were allowed for completion and the GWR stated that no work was to be carried out on a Sunday. A temporary station was used in the interim between the demolition of the original station

GREAT WESTERN RAILWAY.

NOTICE!

COAL.

On and from Monday the 6th instant, and until further Notice, the price of Coal to Company's Servants, Swindon and District,

WILL BE REDUCED FROM
62/6ᴰ TO 47/6ᴰ PER TON,
i.e. 3/1½ᴰ TO 2/4½ᴰ PER CWT.

BY ORDER.

Chief Mechanical Engineer's Dept.
SWINDON.
th December, 1926.

No.   (3305)

GREAT WESTERN RAILWAY.

Swindon Works, 15th August 1930.

908 W. J. HORSE.   *Your services will not*

be required after 5/30pm. Friday 12/9/30.

Manager.

PRIVATE AND NOT FOR PUBLICATION.   NOTICE No. 27.

BRITISH RAILWAYS
(WESTERN OPERATING AREA)

NOTICE
OF
Special Arrangements
IN CONNECTION WITH
SWINDON WORKS
Annual Holiday
1957
(FRIDAY, 5th JULY, TO MONDAY, 22nd JULY)

ALL LOADED SPECIAL PASSENGER TRAINS AND EMPTY STOCK TRAINS (EXCEPT WHERE OTHERWISE INDICATED) SHEWN IN THIS NOTICE MUST CARRY "A" HEAD CODE.

THE TRAINS MUST BE PROPERLY MARSHALLED, CLEANED AND LAVATORIES FULLY EQUIPPED, AND EACH PORTION OF THE FORWARD TRAINS LABELLED ACCORDING TO DESTINATION BEFORE EMPTY COACHES LEAVE THE RESPECTIVE DEPOTS WITH LABELS WHICH THE CHIEF MECHANICAL AND ELECTRICAL ENGINEER WILL SUPPLY TO THE DEPOT AFFECTED. FORWARD AND RETURN TRAINS (ENGINES AND COACHES) MUST BEAR THE TRAIN NUMBER AS SHEWN IN THIS PROGRAMME. TRAINS FORMED AT SWINDON WILL BE LABELLED BY THE C. & W. DEPARTMENT.

Swindon Station Master to wire "MOTIVE," Newton Abbot, and Station Master, Newton Abbot, load in tons of each Down special in that direction, shewing each portion separately.

TELEPHONIC ADVICES OF THE RUNNING OF TRAINS.
It is important that the Standard Instructions in regard to telephonic advices are promptly carried out.

Receipt of this Notice to be acknowledged to Head of Department.

S. G. HEARN,
Chief Operating Superintendent.

PADDINGTON, June, 1957.
T.3948.M.
T.G/869/8.

774

Above: A notice announcing a reduction in the price of coal, 7 December 1926.
(*Author's Collection*)

Top right: A curt notice of dismissal at the end of an apprenticeship, 16th August 1930.
(*Author's Collection*)

Right: Notice of Special Arrangements for Swindon Works Annual Holiday, 1957.
(*Author's Collection*)

12

I, the undersigned, having been appointed as *Boy* in the service of the Great Western Railway Company, do hereby bind myself to observe and obey the foregoing Rules and Regulations; and hereby declare that I have carefully read them (or have had them read to me), and that I clearly understand them and have received a copy of the same.

As witness my hand this *19th* day of *July* 19 09.

Signature *H. R. E. Jarvis*

Witness to Signature } *G. H. Webb*

GREAT WESTERN RAILWAY

RULES AND REGULATIONS

TO BE OBSERVED BY

WORKMEN EMPLOYED IN THE WORKSHOPS

OF THE

LOCOMOTIVE, CARRIAGE AND WAGON DEPARTMENTS.

1. Every applicant for employment must be in good health, and will only be temporarily engaged until a satisfactory character has been received from his last employer for whom he has worked six months. He must produce his Certificate of Birth, and must sign a declaration that he has read a copy of these Rules, and that he undertakes to observe and be bound by them as a condition of his employment. *Condition of Service*

2. The usual hours of work are as follow :— *Hours of work.*

Monday to Friday
{ 6.0 a.m. to 8.15 a.m.
9.0 ,, ,, 1. 0 p.m.
2.0 p.m. ,, 5.30 p.m.

Saturdays ...
{ 6.0 a.m. to 8.15 a.m.
9.0 ,, ,, 12. 0 noon

totalling 54 hours per week, or an average of nine hours per day.

2

Overtime will be reckoned after 5.30 p.m. each day, except Saturday, when it will be reckoned after 12.0 noon. It will be valued at the rate of time and quarter up to 10.0 p.m., and time and half after that hour. This clause applies only to men who have worked the full number of hours during the day.

Men not regularly employed on Sunday duty will be paid for Sunday work at the rate of time and half.

No overtime will be allowed until 54 hours per week have been made, except when work is stopped by reason of accidents to machinery, or when a man has, under pressure of work, worked all the previous night, or when the works are closed at holiday times; Sunday work to stand by itself.

Gas makers, Furnacemen, and others whose ordinary working hours do not correspond with this rule, will be paid according to arrangements made to suit the circumstances of each case.

Sick and Medical Fund Societies. 3. Every workman is required, as a condition of Service, to become a Member of the G.W.R. Medical Fund Society, for providing medicines and medical attendance for the members and their families, and a member of the G.W.R. Sick Fund Society, unless he is already in Benefit Societies

3

which provide adequate sick benefit in case of sickness.

NOTE.—*This rule applies to Swindon Works only.*

4. The engagement to be terminable by 9 working hours' notice on either side. In case of misconduct the workman will be liable to instant dismissal. *Resignation and dismissal.*

5. Any workman absent from the works more than ¼ day, whether from illness or otherwise, must notify the Foreman of the shop, stating the cause of absence. *Absence from duty.*

Any workman absent from work for two days without leave, will be considered as having left the Service, as from the commencement of the absence.

Any workman absent from duty through lead poisoning, must at once inform his Foreman, so that the case may be reported to H.M. Factory Inspector.

6. Each workman will be provided with a number which will be stamped upon the metal ticket, or time recording card supplied. He must place the ticket in the box provided for the purpose each time he enters the works. Workmen who are required to record their time by Time Recorders must strictly observe the instructions laid down for the use of the machines. *Time tickets and time recorders.*

Rules and regulations, 1904, for workmen employed at Swindon Works.

Wootton Bassett, view of Up, *c.* 1880. The goods shed is to the left and the passenger station beyond, with the cottage-like signal-box on the right. The original print shows a mixture of slotted semaphore and disc- and crossbar signals above the signal-box. Notice the horse shunting and the mixed-gauge track.

(Author's Collection)

and the completion of the new. The GWR laid Up and Down refuge sidings either side of both main lines.

Country lorry services started from the station in 1928. Goods traffic chiefly consisted of coal, fertiliser, grain, cattle cake, livestock and timber. As the main lines were on a gradient of 1 in 660 down, the *Appendix to Section 4 of the Working Time Table* of May 1931 stated that 'The greatest possible care must be exercised by each member of staff in carrying out Shunting Operations'. If a vehicle had to be detached on the main line, unless a locomotive was coupled to its rear, handbrakes had to be screwed down before it was uncoupled, while a vehicle without handbrakes had to be placed in a siding before being detached. A brake stick and two hand scotches were required to be kept at each end of the Down platform 'for immediate use if required'. Today, Johnson Aggregates has a siding served by Mendip Rail.

At one time mail-exchange apparatus was situated on the Up side 440 yd east of the station, and also at Chippenham 660 yd west of the station on the Down side, and at Corsham 910 yd east of the station on the Up side.

Staff at Wootton Bassett on 20 December 1920 consisted of: a stationmaster, 1 clerk, 1 goods checker class 2, 2 parcels porters, 3 shunters class 4, 2 porters, 11 signalmen, 1 district lampman and 1 supernumerary for cleaning the cattle pens.

The whistle codes for approaching Down trains were: Main line 1; Badminton line 2. Drivers of the Up trains running non-stop through Swindon, when passing Wootton Bassett were required to give two long whistles and one crow.

Wootton Bassett, view Down, just prior to the opening of the Badminton line on 1 January 1903.
Notice the very attractive GWR monogram on both sides of the bridge and the circles on the inside
displaying the building date of 1890.

(Author's Collection)

'Star' class 4–6–0 No. 4062 *Malmesbury Abbey* with the 4.07 p.m. Swindon to Bristol Temple Meads
stopping train, passing the postal nets at Chippenham West in the early 1950s. The formation and length of
this train demanded expert driving skill in stopping, especially at the short platforms of the three halts.

(Kenneth Leech/P.Q. Treloar Collection)

Wootton Bassett 4 April 2002. Left to right: Up Refuge Siding, the Badminton line and the Chippenham line.

(C.G. Maggs)

The junction originally had a fixed diamond crossing with a limit of 40 mph on the Down Badminton line, but in 1927 it was relaid with movable elbows to the diamond crossing permitting 50 mph. In 1965 it was realigned to allow 70 mph for the Badminton line; for Chippenham trains the limit of 90 mph remained.

Like all stations between Swindon and Bath, except Chippenham and Bathampton, Wootton Bassett closed on 4 October 1965, when stopping passenger services were withdrawn.

Dauntsey Bank is a 1 mile 550 yd descent at 1 in 100, which provided opportunities for steam-hauled expresses to reach speeds in excess of 90 mph. From the embankment there are splendid views over the upper part of the Avon Valley. If a banker was needed, one was sent from Wootton Bassett, a Swindon engine being kept there for the purpose. In about 1890 an engine was sent each evening from Chippenham to assist the 6.40 p.m. Corsham to Paddington stone train and various other heavy night goods trains.

Dauntsey station, in knapped flint with limestone quoins, although in Brunelian style, was built in 1867–8 to the design of George Drew. Until it opened on 1 February 1868 Wootton Bassett to Chippenham, a distance of 11 miles, was one of the longest stretches of main line in the country without a station. Beyond the ramp at the Down end of the Up platform was a separate short platform for Malmesbury branch trains, with a face for the main line as well as the bay. This platform remained *in situ* until April 1956, and its canopy has seen further service sheltering passengers at Yatton, where it remains to this day.

Staff at Dauntsey on 12 February 1921 consisted of a stationmaster, 1 parcels porter, 1 shunter, 2 porters, 1 lad porter and 4 signalmen. After the abolition of junction status, in 1933 the staff consisted of a stationmaster, 1 Grade 1 porter, 2 porters and 3 signalmen. In 1938 the RAF opened an airfield at Lyneham and a booking clerk was appointed to handle the increased traffic. To avoid congestion at the station at weekends, on Fridays either the booking clerk or the stationmaster went to the airfield to issue tickets.

Milk traffic started in the early 1920s, quantities of milk from the Malmesbury branch plus 300 churns from Dauntsey itself being sufficient to warrant a whole train to the London milk depots.

A water tank on the Down platform was gravity-fed from the Wilts & Berks Canal, an automatic valve preventing overflow. One water crane was situated at the east end of the Up platform and the other at the Bristol end of the Down platform between the footbridge and the road overbridge. It is believed that they were removed following the Malmesbury branch diversion of 1933.

Apart from milk, other traffic despatched included timber, hay, and ponies for South Wales pits, while incoming goods included coal and cattle cake, the latter being stored in a grounded coach and collected by farmer's wagon. Parcels were delivered by a Chippenham-based lorry.

The goods sidings at the Up end of the station were worked from a ground frame, the key of which was kept in the stationmaster's office. The person appointed to use the ground frame was required to inform the signalman by telephone what movements were required. No train was allowed to back from the sidings down the Up line towards the signal-box, nor was a train allowed to proceed into the section in advance, until the man working the frame had obtained permission from the signalman. Dauntsey closed to goods from 10 June 1963.

Christian Malford Halt opened on 18 October 1926 near the 90 milepost. Its timber-built, 150-ft-long platforms each had a timber-built shelter, and alighting passengers were required to travel in the rear two coaches. The halt was one of the first to be opened to combat bus competition where an existing station was inconveniently sited. Construction cost about £650 and electric lighting was authorised in 1937 at an estimated cost of £127, including a time switch. The halt was staffed by a porter from 9.30 a.m. to 6 p.m.,

Dauntsey, view Down, 23 August 1955. Notice the Up platform divided by the overbridge.
A green GPO telephone van stands in the station drive, with a telephone engineer up the pole.

(C.G. Maggs)

Christian Malford Halt, view Up, 23 May 1963. The platform and waiting shelters are of timber.
The Down line still has bullhead rail.

(C.G. Maggs)

The Avon Viaduct, 4 April 2002.

(C.G. Maggs)

42XX class 2–8–0T No. 4291 at Langley Crossing, 1955.

(T.J. Saunders)

Mondays to Saturdays, and outside these times the guard collected the tickets. When Up and Down passenger trains stopped simultaneously, the guard of the Down train was required to collect the tickets and hand them to the porter. On 1 December 1954 the halt became unstaffed and was supervised by Chippenham and Dauntsey stations, a lad porter from Chippenham brushing out the shelters weekly. South of the halt the main line crosses the 72-yd-long Avon Viaduct constructed of brick. When multiple aspect signalling was introduced on 4 December 1966, Langley Crossing signal-box closed and the gates were replaced with automatic half barriers: the crossing closed completely in February 1978.

The original Italianate-style, Brunel-designed station at Chippenham, executed in Bath stone, had a low-pitched roof forming a platform canopy on all four sides. The principal buildings, now Grade II listed, are on what was the Down platform. The opening of lines to Salisbury and Weymouth from Thingley Junction in 1856–7 required Chippenham station to be enlarged to cope with the increased traffic. The work was carried out by Rowland Brotherhood. A Down bay and island platform were built and a train shed added to mark its enhanced status. An unusual feature of the train shed was that by 1898 its ends differed in design: that at the east was closed in above roof level, a glass draught-screen shielding part of the platform, while the west end was completely open. The train shed was removed in about 1905. Later an Up bay platform was added for Calne branch trains. In 1900 the Weymouth bay platform was made a through road. However, as it was controlled by Chippenham East and Chippenham West signal-boxes, in order to avoid special permissive block working this through line later had back-to-back

Chippenham station, view Up, 1841. Notice the short platforms and water crane. The goods shed is on the left.

(Author's Collection)

Chippenham, *c.* 1898. A Down train enters the station, with a crowd waiting to board. The Weymouth bay, with timber platform, is on the left. Notice the far end of the train shed is closed above train level, and also the provision of clerestory windows to the Down platform.

(Author's Collection)

buffer stops erected, dividing it into a Weymouth bay and a siding with the delightful name of New-Found-Out. With dieselisation this latter siding became redundant and was lifted on 23 April 1964, as was the Weymouth bay on 21 August 1966. On 1 February 1976 the Down main line was slewed to the south side of the island platform in preparation for HST running. In 1990 the station, Wiltshire's third-busiest, was cleaned and modernised, with 200 extra car parking spaces being created in the old goods yard, raising the total to 650. About a thousand passengers commuted to London daily, each paying £3,308 for a season ticket.

The stone-walled, two-road goods shed, 194 ft in length, contained three 2-ton cranes. At its west end were workshops for permanent-way carpenters, painters and plumbers. This lean-to shop was demolished in about 1947 when the goods shed was modified so that Royal Navy trailers from Hawthorn could be backed at right angles to the loading platform. The goods shed itself was demolished in about 1976 in order to extend the station car park. Goods traffic ceased entirely on 1 January 1981.

Between the goods shed and the station entrance in Cocklebury Road was a milk shed open on one side for lorry access. Ten vans of Nestlé's milk left each night for Brentford Dock, and the shed was also used for unloading tinplate for the Nestlé factory. Sacks of sugar were also unloaded, as was timber for making boxes in which to pack the cans of

A train of broad-gauge locomotives en route for conversion or scrapping at Swindon, May 1892.
The leading engine is 3001 class 2–2–2 No. 3024, built in July 1891, converted to standard gauge
in August 1892 and reconstructed as a 4–2–2 named *Storm King* in December 1894.

(P.Q. Treloar Collection)

Chippenham, view Down, Easter 1937. An auto coach and gas cylinder wagon stand in the
New-Found-Out Siding, an 0–4–2T and van are in the Fish Dock, and a coach and van in the Parcels Dock.

(M.J. Tozer)

condensed milk. Brooke Bond had a tea depot in the station yard east of the goods depot
and local deliveries were made by a Trojan van.

The station attracted considerable industry close by: a foundry, brewery, cheese factory,
bacon factory, gasworks and stone works, as well as coal, salt and hay merchants. The
bacon siding agreement terminated on 1 September 1964, while the gasworks had closed
on 16 December 1932.

The railway building and maintenance contractor Rowland Brotherhood had his
railway works at Chippenham, constructing small locomotives, railway coaches, tilts for
railway wagons and general railway fittings. He ceased trading in about 1870, following
his overstretched credit from 1865–6, but continued with minor contracts after 1870. In
1870 the GWR directors authorised their locomotive superintendent Joseph Armstrong
to rent temporary premises 'lately belonging to Mr Brotherhood', to be used as carriage
sheds at a rental of £120 per annum. In 1895 these works were taken over by Evans,
O'Donnell & Company, signal engineers who by 1900 had a workforce of 200 making
signals and pneumatic tools. In 1903 the company was bought by Saxby & Farmer of
Kilburn, which then transferred its works to Chippenham. In 1920 it amalgamated with
the Westinghouse Power Signal Company to become the Westinghouse Brake & Saxby
Signal Company Limited, and in 1935 the Westinghouse Brake & Signal Company
Limited. In 1952 the Westinghouse owned 46 acres. By 1960 the works had diversified
into manufacturing brakes for road vehicles, semi-conductors, rectifiers and equipment
for the remote control of gas, water, oil and electricity supplies. As the company

Chippenham, view Up, *c*. 1923.
The Wiltshire Bacon Curing Company
factory is on the far left.

(P.C. Mortimore Collection)

Saxby & Farmer's cast-iron maker's plate.

(Author's Collection)

No. 5077 *Eastnor Castle* leaves Chippenham with the 7.55 a.m. Taunton–Paddington during 1939.
The 10.23 a.m. passenger service to Calne is on the left. SR cattle wagons for Chippenham market traffic
are on the right. In October 1940 No. 5077 was renamed *Fairey Battle* in honour of a fighter bomber
used in the Battle of Britain.

(E.J.M. Hayward)

expanded it took in Hathaway's works, which had manufactured milk and butter churns
and other dairy appliances. Its private siding agreement terminated on 30 June 1976.

Cattle were despatched after the Friday market at Chippenham, the 5 p.m.
Chippenham to Bristol East depot pick-up goods being up-rated that day to a non-stop
vacuum-fitted goods comprised mainly of cattle trucks and headed by anything from a
pannier tank to a 'Hall'. During the Second World War Chippenham goods yard was
tremendously busy because, apart from the needs of the town, there were nearby
ammunition stores, RAF camps and an RN depot to service. In addition to the hardware
sent to and from these units, fruit, fish, vegetables, Lyons' cakes and ice cream were
required for the RAF camps.

Horses were used for goods delivery in the town and motor lorries for the environs,
and a Morris Commercial motor express cartage van, with sliding cab doors, was used
for parcels delivery from the parcels office. GWR motor lorries first appeared in
Chippenham in about 1918, and by 1924 solid-tyre AEC and Thornycroft vehicles were
in use delivering to Castle Combe, Colerne, Dauntsey, Luckington, Lyneham and Yatton
Keynell. In 1939 a Scammell mechanical horse with about eight trailers was used for
town deliveries, but was later replaced by two 6-tonners.

Westinghouse was a good customer, one GWR vehicle being kept busy shuttling
between the works and station with small packages, with only large items using the
private siding. The Nestlé milk factory also kept a GWR horse and cart, or motor lorry,
busy. In the 1940s Chippenham employed about six lorry drivers and two horse drivers.

The staff on 20 November 1920 consisted of a stationmaster, chief clerk, 1 parcels clerk, 2 male booking clerks, 1 female booking clerk, 4 passenger guards, 3 goods guards, 4 goods shunters class 2, 3 goods shunters class 4, 2 passenger shunters, 12 signalmen, 1 signal lampman, 3 ticket collectors, 2 passenger foremen, 4 parcels porters, 1 porter-guard, 7 porters and 1 female waiting room attendant. In the post-Second World War era there were sufficient railwaymen at Chippenham to form a football team, the Railway Ramblers, who played at Cocklebury in a field almost opposite Chippenham East signal-box, from where the signalman cheered them on through his megaphone, normally used for shouting instructions to drivers.

A water tank supplied the water columns and the station's non-drinking water taps. Until replaced by an electric pump in about 1938, a steam-pump for filling the tank was situated in a road called Foghamshire, the full-time pumper living in a company house on the opposite side of the road.

As the footwarmer room at the east end of the Down platform heated only six to ten containers daily, and consumed 8 cwt of coal weekly, as an economy measure it was discontinued in 1906 and footwarmers obtained at Swindon or Bristol.

On 30 October 1858 Joseph Hill and William Powell, woolstaplers from London, were summoned on a charge of 'perniciously smoking in one of the Company's carriages' on

GWR Chippenham District St John's Ambulance class at Chippenham, April 1922.
Note the first-aid cabinet and stretcher in the foreground.

(Author's Collection)

45XX class 2–6–2T No. 4569 being watered at Chippenham, *c.* 1962. It is coupled to an ER parcels van.

(Christopher Kent)

No. 1011, formerly named *County of Chester*, propels a Down pick-up freight into the Down sidings,
27 October 1964. It had been used on an enthusiasts' special, which explains the number on the buffer beam.

(Christopher Kent)

The Central Ammunition Depot sidings, Thingley Junction, view Up, 4 August 1959. Centre left can be seen what is believed to be an ex-Metropolitan Railway car, built in 1905.

(C.G. Maggs)

'Dean Goods' class 0–6–0 No. 2445 with an Up train at Thingley Junction, *c.* 1952. No. 2445 was withdrawn in March 1953.

(T.J. Saunders)

Brown-Boveri gas turbine No. 18000, now preserved at The Railway Age, Crewe, passes Thingley Junction with a Down express, *c.* 1951. On the far left is a Thingley Junction RU (restricted use) brake van.

(T.J. Saunders)

2 September, contrary to bye-laws. At Temple Meads a guard saw them smoking and asked them to desist. This warning was received with ridicule. The guard found them still smoking at Chippenham and, on remonstrating with them, Hill blew a puff of smoke in his face. The defendants were fined £1 each plus costs. A charge against another member of the party was arranged out of court by payment of the full penalty of £2 plus costs.

The Chippenham to Bath section required the heaviest engineering works. The Grade II listed 90-yd-long Chippenham Viaduct is immediately west of the station, followed by a high embankment for more than 2 miles, then 3 miles of deep cutting to Corsham, followed by Box and Middle Hill tunnels. Chippenham Viaduct today is somewhat spoilt by strengthening rings, but a redeeming feature is that they taper into the piers. Rowland Brotherhood's Regency-style house, how a bed shop, is on the south side of the viaduct. In about 1900 one of the viaduct arches was converted into a gymnasium.

Thingley Junction, colloquially 'Thingley Jungle', 2 miles south-west of Chippenham, is where the Wilts, Somerset & Weymouth Railway branch to Trowbridge diverges. With the area around Corsham being developed for ammunition storage, and Corsham station being in a cutting and therefore making it difficult to expand facilities there, in January 1937 an Up and Down goods loop, plus eleven sidings for the reception and despatch of ammunition, were opened at Thingley Junction on the north side of the main line. Following a decrease in traffic, some of the sidings were taken out of use in 1966. Seven remain today, Rail & Marine Engineering Limited having purchased the 100-acre site from the Ministry of Defence in 1995. Following the Hatfield derailment and the subsequent large-scale rail renewal required in 2001, the sidings were used for butt welding new rail into 240 ft lengths.

A short distance west of these sidings were Air Ministry sidings controlled by a new signal-box, Thingley West Junction, opened on 2 September 1943, while the double-track Air Ministry Loop, in use from 2 September 1943 to 20 February 1955, formed a triangular junction with the Trowbridge line. There is little trace of the latter today. Between Thingley Junction and Thingley West boxes, an Up and Down goods running loop was worked as a single line without staff. The Thingley Junction boxes had better facilities than most, enjoying mains water and drainage and electric light. A disadvantage was that they faced north and were very cold, being in an open situation.

As Corsham station was situated in a cutting, each platform merely had a waiting shelter, while the office building in Pound Mead was at the top of the cutting. Rowland Brotherhood lengthened the platforms in November 1875. The goods sidings and stone wharf were to the west. The cutting of Box Tunnel revealed large supplies of building stone in the area and the GWR provided a ready means of transport. By 1864 100,000 tons of stone were despatched by rail from Corsham station annually, being sold at Birmingham for 1s 5d per cubic foot, in Plymouth for 1s 4d, and in Newcastle for 1s 7d, while the local price was 6d. Randell & Saunders commenced in 1845 and Pictor & Sons also opened about the same time, both firms forming a consortium, Bath Stone Firms Ltd, in 1887.

Stone was not quarried in low, dark tunnels like a coal mine, but in wide, lofty, well-ventilated and well-lit tunnels. All these earlier workings were on the north side of Box railway tunnel, the quarry entrance being beside the main line at the eastern portal of the GWR's tunnel. Inside it divided into Box Hill Quarry and Corsham Down Quarry, respectively on the west and east sides of the hill. Wagons on the 2 ft 6 in gauge internal tramways gravitated to a loading platform about 220 yd from the tunnel entrance.

43XX class 2–6–0 No. 6347 (87H, Neyland), making a rare appearance in the area, passes Thingley Junction signal-box with a Down freight, *c.* 1952. The open wagon behind the tender is a three-plank dropside with 'LMS' in large lettering.

(T.J. Saunders)

Corsham goods yard, view Up, *c.* 1910. Notice the blocks of stone on the wharf awaiting transhipment by crane, the 2 ft 6 in gauge stone tramway tracks on the wharf, and the Aveling & Porter roadroller.

(Author's Collection)

The Up goods platform in the foreground, *c.* 1910, with the stone wharf on the far side of the main line. Stone awaits loading into Marsh Son & Gibbs Ltd, Box, and Bath Stone Firms, dumb-buffer low-sided wagons.

(Author's Collection)

Corsham Quarry Company wagon No. 70, built by the Gloucester Railway Carriage & Wagon Company Ltd in August 1899. It bore a red livery with white letters shaded black.

(Author's Collection)

A triple-headed stone train on the stone tramway, *c.* 1905.

(Author's Collection)

To ease transfer by crane, tramway wagons on the loading platform were at the same height as the floor of a broad-gauge wagon. One crane would load up to 400 tons of stone in 10 hours. The average tonnage produced daily was 340. Forty-six broad-gauge wagons were owned by Randell & Saunders but GWR wagons carried the largest proportion of the traffic. Although stone was excavated all year, May to Christmas was the time when most orders were received. Box Tunnel East signal-box controlled the siding, closed on 24 June 1910, though other access had been made back in 1876 when the siding was extended to the goods yard at Corsham. Three or four times daily horses worked main-line wagons to and from the tunnel and Corsham under the control of Box Tunnel East signal-box.

A network of horse-worked 2 ft 6 in gauge tramways linked other stone quarries with the wharf at Corsham station. From 1931 a Muir-Hill four-wheeled petrol-mechanical engine, works No. L108, worked the Park Lane Quarry line. The tramways were closed in 1939 and lifted. From early in the twentieth century stone traffic had decreased and continued to decrease during the stagnation of the building trade following the First World War and the introduction of United States' tariff barriers during the Depression. Some stone continued to be loaded on to rail at Corsham until about 1960. Two handcranes transferred stone from lorry to railway wagon. On one occasion when porter Frank Davis was working a crane, the ratchet slipped, the handle spun and he received severe bruising.

In about 1855 a gasworks was built on the north side of the line and tar was piped down to the station. The local company was taken over by the Bath Gas Company and the works closed on 16 December 1932.

On the Up side coal wagons used the mileage road leading to the goods shed, while on the Down side was the Back Road serving the stone wharf, then the Middle Road, while beside the main line was 'The Straight'. Latterly two motor vans were kept at Corsham, one for town delivery and one for country. In about 1958 approximately six coal wagons, each carrying about 9 tons, arrived for coal merchant H. Blake and another six for W.V. Hancock & Son.

During the Second World War a buffer depot holding emergency food supplies for the area was established at Potley. Items stored there included grain. One signalman at Corsham rented about ¾ acre of GWR land opposite the signal-box for growing vegetables and keeping hens and geese. Grain spillage was part of his poultry feed.

Corsham station closed to coal and freight from 10 June 1963, but the stone-built goods shed still stands today.

On 15 March 1922 Corsham staff consisted of a stationmaster, 1 clerk, 1 junior clerk, 3 signalmen, 1 parcels porter, 1 shunter, 2 porters and 1 lad porter. As the last ammunition was despatched in February 1922 from storage in a local quarry, the employment of a shunter was no longer justified and the post abolished. Using a handcart, the lad porter delivered parcels within a mile radius of the station and the daily average of fifteen parcels was despatched at 10.30 a.m., noon, 2 p.m. and 3.30 p.m. The 1922 report recommended that these deliveries be reduced to two. His duties also included assisting with the station lamps.

	1922 staff costs	Proposed costs
	£	£
Stationmaster	286	286
Clerk	140	140
Junior clerk	115	–
Shunter	149 10s	–
Parcels porter	152 2s	152 2s
2 porters (total)	275 12s	413 8s (for 3 porters)
Lad porter	81 18s	–
	1,200 2s	991 10s

In February 1912 the senior goods clerk at Corsham was discharged. He had a receipt book not supplied to the station which he had used when collecting payment from GWR customers. He kept only a few pounds, 'to meet his liabilities', being slightly in arrears with household payments and was also pressed by tradesmen.

No barrow crossing was provided at the passenger station; fifty porters were faced with the arduous task of pushing barrows up and down a very steep slope. When George Marsh, the local fish, fruit and vegetable merchant, received goods from the 'Calne Bunk' which reversed at Box, it would have been easier to unload it at the Up platform on its return, but as Marsh required the produce at the earliest possible moment it had to be unloaded on the Down platform and carted across.

The fact that the station was situated away from the town centre and located in a cutting did not deter passengers in the early days, the *Bath Chronicle* of 20 July 1843 recording: 'Notwithstanding the present inconvenience at the Railway Station at Corsham, the number of passengers who are taken up and put down at the above-named place surprises the most sanguine.' In December 1879, when the lake in Corsham Park froze, Lord Methuen allowed people to skate on it, and in addition to the scheduled service to Corsham the GWR specially stopped some expresses for skaters, several hundred passengers arriving daily.

Corsham was one of the more luxurious signal-boxes, having running water, while electric light was installed in the box and station in about 1963. Because it faced south, the sun shining in made it difficult to read the instruments on the shelf, so the upper windows were painted cream. The Up distant signal, merely an armless spectacle plate, was situated in Box Tunnel, 1,547 yd from Corsham signal-box. Although the Down distant was 1,787 yd away, that in the tunnel was harder to pull because of the damp conditions.

When not in use, the key to the locks securing the two rail blocks and gate near Quarry Tunnel was required to be kept in Corsham signal-box. The quarry company, after the loaded trucks were worked away, had to leave sufficient room inside the gate for not less than twelve empty wagons to stand. The stone company undertook not to allow their horse or horses when moving trucks to go beyond the gate, but if it was necessary to work down extra trucks which had been left on the station side of the gate and a GWR engine was unavailable to push them inside, a GWR servant would be sent down to unlock the gate and blocks to enable the stone company's horse, by means of a tow rope, to draw the empties inside the enclosure without the animal having to go outside the gate.

Corsham station was the site of an amazing scene on 25 June 1935. Between 2.45 p.m. and 5 p.m. a terrific storm occurred and the Yockney Brook burst its bank just before it entered the timber and bitumen aqueduct which crosses the GWR west of the station.

Corsham signal-box, c. 1964. The breeze block surround at the foot of the steps is for ash storage.
A lagged water pipe may just be discerned at the rear of the signal-box. On the right-hand corner
is a white mark indicating the height of the 1935 flood.

(Christopher Kent)

Workmen at the east portal of Box Tunnel, probably in June 1906, when it was closed for repair.

(Clive Hancock Collection)

The flooded yard, viewed from the footbridge, 25 June 1935.

(Norman Whalley Collection)

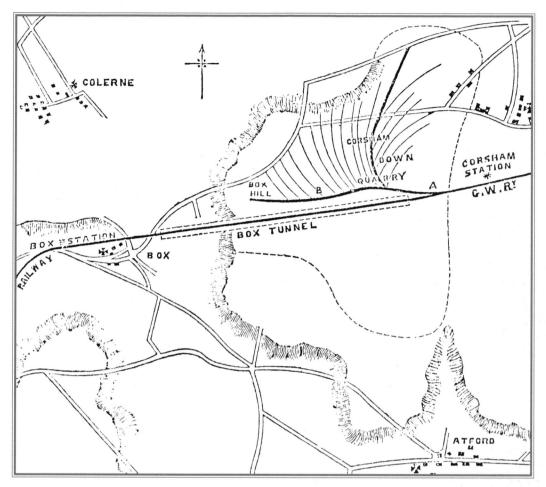

Map showing Box Tunnel and Bath stone workings under Box Hill. The modern name of the village in the lower right-hand corner is 'Atworth'.

(The Builder, 1862)

The last train before the flood was the 3.15 p.m. Chippenham to Bath, due at Corsham at 3.23 p.m., and within 10 minutes of its departure the water was level with the Down platform, having risen 3 ft 6 in in that brief time. Just after 4 p.m. the water started to rise so quickly that it stretched for 350 yd through the station. On the Down platform the water was 9 ft deep and covered seats in the waiting room. The water caused a landslide behind the signal-box, earth and water falling on an adjacent hut and smashing two bicycles inside. The signalman was marooned for two hours, with turbulent water swirling round his box. All electrical equipment, including the telephone, was put out of action. The stationmaster, E.C. Saxon, who visited the box at 4.30 p.m., was trapped for half an hour before escaping through a window and up the bank to the road above. Water rose nearly to the top of the stone wagons in the siding opposite. Box Tunnel was not flooded because the railway rises at 1 in 660 from the station almost to the east portal. Trains were diverted via Badminton or Bradford-on-Avon.

Passengers at Bath sitting in the 4.47 p.m. Bath to Chippenham train were asked their destination and those for Box and Corsham were informed that the railway was blocked.

The stationmaster speedily procured a bus for them, but on reaching Lambridge on the outskirts of Bath, the road was found to be flooded. It then attempted to go via Larkhall, but encountered more floods. The bus returned to Bath station, where more passengers were waiting, so a second bus was procured. Both buses went up Lansdown Hill to Wick and reached Corsham via Marshfield and Biddestone. The Box contingent eventually arrived home at 8.30 p.m. instead of 4.59 p.m. Next morning they were picked up by bus and reached Bath by the direct route. The first train to pass through Corsham after the flood left Chippenham at 11.07 a.m. on 26 June and was an excursion carrying several hundred Sunday school children from Calne to Weston-super-Mare. The 9.15 a.m. Paddington to Weston-super-Mare left Chippenham soon after.

Just before daybreak on 10 October 1935 another storm flooded the line at Corsham for 200 yd, and from 5.30 a.m. till 8.30 a.m. passengers were conveyed between Chippenham and Bath and vice versa by a fleet of buses chartered by the GWR.

However, this type of event was not altogether uncommon, as on 24 October 1882 Herbert Spackman had written in his diary: 'Water nearly up to the platform at Corsham station. The water was falling in about a dozen streams near the aqueduct and looked very pretty.' On the signal-box a mark, periodically repainted, about 5 ft 4 in above ground level, indicate the height of the June 1935 flood.

Today road traffic into Bath from the east is extremely heavy, especially at peak periods. Since 1988 a pressure group has recommended that Corsham station, which closed to passengers on 4 January 1965, be reopened, but its plans were dashed in May 2003 when the Oxford to Bristol service was withdrawn owing to pressure on line usage. This was the only service which could have called at Corsham.

The aqueduct was originally a single-span structure with stone abutments, and it is believed that when two side spans were added when additional tracks were laid below,

Corsham aqueduct, view Up, with the former goods shed beyond, 14 June 2002.

(C.G. Maggs)

A view through Box Tunnel from the east portal, 16 September 1983. Daylight may just be seen
at the Box end. The tunnel to the ammunition storage depot can be seen on the right.

(John Mann)

the original abutments were converted into piers. The Up side pier is more slender
because the alternative would have been a greater excavation of the rock cutting in order
to secure clearance for the new siding. The timber trough was replaced by one of
reinforced concrete at a cost of £1,900, the work being completed in September 1946.

In 1915 the stone mine at The Ridge, Neston, linked to Corsham station by a 2 ft 6 in
gauge tramway, was used for storing up to 16,000 tons of Tri-Nitro-Toluene and cordite,
the 500 tons despatched daily enjoying the exclusive use of Corsham sidings.

Mining ceased at Tunnel Quarry in about 1930, but with the rise of Hitler the quarry
offered a large area for ammunition storage. As more sidings could not be laid at
Corsham, about 2 million tons of stone debris cleared from Tunnel Quarry was tipped
into GWR 10-ton wagons in the underground siding and 600 tons hauled daily to
Thingley Junction as landfill for new sidings. The Tunnel Quarry was of substandard
height, as hitherto it had only been used by low-sided wagons, but at a cost of £50,000
the roof was raised to allow access by box vans. The low portal had an ornate carved
Bath stone facing which, when the height was increased, was replaced by reinforced
concrete. The railway platform in Tunnel Quarry was lengthened to about 660 ft and
reconditioned in concrete to standard GWR height, and a new line laid to serve its
northern face. It could handle 2,000 tons of ammunition daily. The first ammunition
arrived on 13 July 1938. For safety reasons the War Department agreed not to store
explosives within 100 ft of the main-line tunnel. Transfer of traffic between the WD and
the GWR was normally made just outside the tunnel, though the WD engines were
registered for working over the GWR. During the week ending 19 June 1944 1,100
wagon-loads of ammunition left Thingley Junction.

Anti-tank mine fuses being loaded at the southern face of the loading platform in Tunnel Quarry, 1943.

(Author's Collection)

The WD kept three Hunslet standard-gauge diesel locomotives, Nos 855, 856 and 857, underground at Tunnel Quarry in a three-bay roundhouse. When the engines required major overhaul they were transferred to the Royal Engineers' main workshop at Bicester. The locomotives were constructed for low-height working and had 8-cylinder 204-bhp Gardner engines, and at the time were the largest ever constructed for underground work. The exhaust was conditioned to prevent aldehydes causing acute irritation of the eyes and nose. Tunnel Quarry was emptied of ammunition on 4 December 1962 and the rail connection taken out of use on 28 April 1974.

To the south of the GWR Box Tunnel, but not rail-connected, was Spring Quarry, where there was an underground dispersal factory for the Bristol Aeroplane Company to build Pegasus and Centaurus engines. BSA also occupied part of the site for an Oerlikon gun barrel mill. It was hoped to carry workers from Bristol to the satellite BAC factory by rail, but the line was already intensely used, so a fleet of 120 buses was utilised.

Box Tunnel, 3,212 yd long and 213 ft above sea level at its eastern portal, is on a falling gradient of 1 in 100. It is rumoured that large landowners in the area objected to the planned route, which was to the north of the present line and would have avoided a long tunnel by using the By-brook Valley. The eastern portal is marred by a blue brick lining added in 1895, lowering the roof to standard-gauge dimensions. It can best be seen through binoculars from Potley Lane overbridge.

In May 1842 an eminent geologist, the Revd Dr William Buckland of Oxford and later Dean of Westminster, told the Institution of Civil Engineers he believed that vibration, plus a concussion of air, would cause the oolite in the tunnel to fall. The *Bath Chronicle*, in its issue of 23 June 1842, poured scorn on his theory:

We perceive a paragraph going the round of the papers, stating that Professor Buckland has taken upon himself to pronounce the Box Tunnel is in a dangerous state, and that, at some indefinite space of a time a fearful accident may be anticipated therefrom. We really think it is due to all parties – the directors and proprietors of, and the passengers upon, the magnificent Great Western line, that the learned professor should be somewhat more specific in his charges and in his remedies. For ourselves, remembering the confident predictions of another great luminary in science that steam communication with America was perfectly impossible, we have no great faith in these abstract speculations. We would infinitely rather rely on the judgment of a practical engineer like Mr Brunel, than on the guesses of a theoretical philosopher.

Nevertheless, Maj. Gen. Pasley of the Board of Trade made an inspection on 11 August 1842 accompanied by Mr Merchant, one of Brunel's assistants, and Mr Brewer, quarry owner and contractor. The ½-mile-long section of tunnel through the great oolite was unlined and in the shape of a Gothic arch, but that which passed through fuller's earth and inferior oolite had between four and seven concentric rings of brick, and nine at the western entrance. Except where the great oolite formed the foundation for the bottom of the tunnel, an inverted arch was used. Some side walls through parts of the inferior oolite were left unbricked, but when passing through this rock the roof was always bricked. Pasley found the brickwork 'well-executed' and the blue lias mortar 'of excellent quality'.

Pasley made a thorough inspection, striking the great oolite with a hammer or with an iron rod, and 'everywhere emitted a clear, sharp sound', thus indicating that it was secure. He also visited underground quarries. These had a flat roof spanning up to 29 ft without support. Pasley concluded the Gothic arch of Box Tunnel to be a safer shape than the flat roof of the quarries and, as the latter had been safe for years, even with their vertical cracks from which the tunnel was free, Pasley concluded the tunnel to be safe.

In respect of the supposed concussion of air produced by locomotives passing through the tunnel which Buckland had claimed was dangerous, Pasley stood 3 to 4 ft from two passenger trains and one goods train passing through the tunnel, 'and nearer to him than any rock', yet he found 'not the smallest personal inconvenience'.

A severe frost on 24 March 1845 caused some scaling and a 3-cwt rock fell 160 yd west of No. 7 shaft, where a temporary air shaft made during construction had been blocked up. It fell only a few feet in front of a banker returning 'light engine', derailing it. Workmen clearing the line shortly after were alarmed by two other falls, one of about a ton and another of 12 cwt. The principal cause of the collapse was frost disintegrating stone around an inadequately sealed vent shaft. Three brick arches were made beneath this blocked air shaft and also that of main shaft No. 7, the latter being filled. That year Pasley brought Dr Buckland to Box Tunnel. Dr Buckland spent several hours tapping and left convinced that the tunnel was indeed safe.

The tunnel was closed for five weeks following a fall, again caused by frost, of 700 tons on 23 February 1895, while more of its length was lined. Traffic in the interim was diverted via Bradford-on-Avon. A hundred men were employed laying the east curve on the formation at Bradford Junction, enabling diverted trains to run without reversal from Bathampton to Chippenham. The curve opened on 10 March 1895. The workmen who repaired the tunnel were taken from their task of improving Bath station, but resumed there on 24 March 1895.

On Sunday night, 1 July 1906, a mass of slimy blue clay, estimated to weigh 600 tons, fell and piled almost to the tunnel roof, so again traffic was diverted. The fall was noticed by the district permanent way inspector, C.E. Baughan. It broke the electric alarm wires which gave warning in adjacent signal-boxes. Spoil removal was not completed until 4 July, when engineer's trains could be run, with 105 ft length of timber staging to support the tunnel and three rows of vertical timber baulks – two rows in the 4-ft way between the rails and the tunnel sides, and the third in the 6-ft way between the Up and Down roads. These three rows supported a platform 15 ft above the tracks, allowing trains to pass below. The tunnel lining was replaced in brick and concrete, and the cavity from which the clay fell was filled with faggots.

On Sunday 8 July the roof and sides of the tunnel were inspected by J.R. Godsall of Bristol using a travelling crane with a cage fixed to its jib, in which were three navvies armed with crowbars. They probed brickwork while passing to discover any further weaknesses. A tank containing compressed oil gas was attached to the crane and a flexible hose connection enabled light to be available for inspection. To facilitate repair a temporary telephone was fitted in the tunnel, and electric gongs worked from signal-boxes gave workers warning of approaching trains.

On Thursday 19 July the Up line opened for traffic, but Down passenger traffic continued to travel via Bradford-on-Avon. Down goods traffic was permitted to pass through the tunnel, but the timber staging was so close to the Down line that it was considered undesirable to allow passenger trains through. With the reopening to Up trains, a spare engine was kept at Bath to assist all trains hauled by an engine with a single pair of driving wheels. This precaution was essential because, had a stop been required, a 'single' locomotive would have experienced difficulty in restarting on the gradient. The Down line reopened at 6 a.m. on 31 July, though repair work was still incomplete.

In March 1917 Box Tunnel was closed for further relining, some trains being diverted via Bradford-on-Avon and others through Badminton. Questions were asked in Parliament as fares were increased owing to the longer distance travelled between stations because of the diversion. The price of a Chippenham to Bath return rose from 2s 2d to 4s 7d and from Corsham to Bath from 1s 3d to 4s 7d. The Board of Trade secured a reduction to 2s 6d from Corsham, but not from Chippenham.

The tunnel was the scene of a curious mishap on 15 October 1910. 4–4–0 No. 3433 *City of Bath*, working the 9 a.m. Temple Meads to Paddington, had lost 10 minutes at Bath as it was required to pick up a horsebox from the middle road to add to the seven bogie coaches. Seeking to make up time, No. 3433's driving wheels slipped in the tunnel and before Driver Edward Ash could close the regulator, one wheel became welded to the rail. This caused the left-hand driving crank pin to break, the side rod came off and the right-hand rod buckled. Fireman Bill Dennis broke the telltale wire on the tunnel wall. Driver Ash thoughtfully reassured passengers that it was just a locomotive failure and that they were in no danger. The bank engine, 3521 class 4–4–0 No. 3540, was not immediately available as it had piloted a heavy excursion train to Chippenham. On returning to Box it was sent to the tunnel with a wrong line order and came back with the coaches, which had been in the tunnel for an hour. Fireman Dennis walked through the tunnel to Corsham with a wrong line order to enable breakdown vans to travel down the Up line to rescue No. 3433. The Corsham stationmaster, J. Toy, called from his Sunday worship, travelled to Box on the 9.20 a.m. Paddington to Plymouth to set up single-line working over the Down road. As he arrived at Box the message was received from Corsham that No. 3433's coupling rods had been cut through and the engine drawn from the tunnel.

At 39 ft high and 35 ft wide, Box Tunnel required the excavation of 414,000 cubic yards of material. There are reputed to be a million faggots of wood placed in the roof

GREAT WESTERN RAILWAY.

REDUCED THIRD CLASS RETURN FARES.

Commencing on Tuesday, July 31st, 1906,

The Third Class Return Fares between the following stations will be revised as follows:

	s.	d.		s.	d.
Bath & Box	0	8	Bath & Bradford-on-Avon	1	4
Bath & Corsham	1	3	Bath & Trowbridge	1	9
Bath & Chippenham	1	10	Bath & Melksham	2	3

Bradford-on-Avon & Trowbridge - - - 5d.

NOTE.—In a few cases the SINGLE FARES have also been REDUCED.

The Train Service between BATH and CHIPPENHAM and BATH, TROWBRIDGE and MELKSHAM is as under:—

WEEK-DAYS.

		a.m.	a.m.	a.m.	a.m.	a.m.	a.m.	a.m.	a.m.	a.m.	a.m.	p.m.	p.m.	p.m.		
BATH	dep.	12A42	1B18	7 7	8 2	Sats.	9 2	9 54	10 15	10 38	11 32	1 30	3 30	4 7	..	..
BOX	,,	..	..	7 23	..	except.	9 18	..	10 33	10 54	11 47	1 45	3 44	..	..	..
CORSHAM	,,	..	..	7 34	..	8 30	9 28	..	10 44		11 57	1 55	3 54	..	..	..
CHIPPENHAM	arr.	1A4	1B40	7 42	8 22	8 40	9 37	10 16	10 55		12 5	2 3	4 2	4 30	..	..

WEEK-DAYS.   **SUNDAYS.**

		p.m.	p.m.	p.m.	p.m.	p.m.	p.m.				p.m.	p.m.	p.m.	p.m.	p.m.	
BATH	dep.	5 43	6 54	7 5	8 15	9S31	11W0	..	..	..	12 42	10 32	2 5	6 7	6 28	..
BOX	,,	5 59	7 11	7 22	8 29	9 48	11 14	..	..	..	..	10 47	2 20	..	6 43	..
CORSHAM	,,	6 10	7 22		8 39	9 59	11 24	..	..	..	..	10 57	2 30	..	6 53	..
CHIPPENHAM	arr.	6 18	7 30		8 47	10 7	11 34	..	..	..	1 4	11 5	2 38	6 30	7 1	..

WEEK-DAYS.

		a.m.	a.m.	a.m.	a.m.	a.m.		a.m.	a.m.	p.m.	p.m.	p.m.	p.m.	p.m.	p.m.	
CHIPPENHAM	dep.	6 35	7 47	8 5	8 18	10 0	..	11 24	11 56	12 50	2 5	2S43	3 50	5 0	5 57	..
CORSHAM	,,	6 45	..	8 15	8 28	10 9	..	11 33	12 6	1 1	2 15	2 53	4 0	5 10	6 6	..
BOX	,,	6 54	..	Sats.	8 36	10 17	11 2	11 40	12 14	1 9	2 23	3 1	4 8	4 18	6 14	..
BATH	arr.	7 6	8 5	except.	8 52	10 29	11 15	11 54	12 26	1 21	2 35	3 14	4 21	5 32	6 26	..

WEEK-DAYS.   **SUNDAYS.**

		p.m.	p.m.	p.m.	p.m.	p.m.	p.m.				p.m.	p.m.	p.m.	p.m.	mdnt	
CHIPPENHAM	dep.	..	7 46	8 40	9W50	10 24	12 13	..	..	..	12 20	1 54	6 36	12 13	..	
CORSHAM	,,	..	..	8 51	10 0	..	..	..	..	..	12 20	2 5	6 46	..	..	
BOX	,,	7 35	..	9 0	10 9	..	..	..	..	..	12 39	2 11	6 54	..	..	
BATH	arr.	7 52	8 4	9 13	10 22	10 41	12 31	..	..	..	12 52	2 23	7 7	12 31	..	

WEEK-DAYS.

		a.m.	a.m.	a.m.	a.m.	a.m.	a.m.	noon.	p.m.	p.m.	p.m.	p.m.	p.m.	p.m.	p.m.	
BATH	dep.	6 22	8 39	9 35	10 30	11 9	11 45	12 0	12 20	12 50	1 25	2 45	3 35	4 16	4 30	..
BRADFORD-on-AVON	,,	6 49	9 7	10 2	10 57	..	..	12 16	12 47	..	1 51	3 13	4 3	4 35	4 56	..
TROWBRIDGE	arr.	6 57	9 16	10 10	11 5	11 31	12 6	..	12 51	1 11	1 59	3 22	4 11	4 45	..	
MELKSHAM	arr.	7 53	9 42	11 3	11 35	12 13	12 48	..	1 58	1 58	2 57	4 3	..	5 5	..	

WEEK-DAYS.   **SUNDAYS.**

		p.m.	p.m.	p.m.	p.m.	p.m.	p.m.	p.m.	p.m.	p.m.	a.m.	p.m.	p.m.	p.m.		
BATH	dep.	4 46	5 19	5 27	5 57	6 32	7 20	8 10	9 21	11 27	9 6	2 20	4 17	7 2	..	..
BRADFORD-on-AVON	,,	5 3	..	5 54	..	7 0	7 50	8 35	9 49	Y	9 34	2 46	4 47	7 30	..	..
TROWBRIDGE	arr.	5 11	5 44	6 2	6 19	7 10	8 0	8 43	9 57	11 55	9 42	2 54	4 55	7 38	..	..
MELKSHAM	arr.	5 32	..	6 28	7 3	..	8 43	10 11	12S10	..	1 30	..	5 34	..	..	..

WEEK-DAYS.

		a.m.	a.m.	a.m.	a.m.	a.m.	a.m.	a.m.	p.m.	p.m.	p.m.	p.m.	p.m.	p.m.	p.m.	
MELKSHAM	dep.	6 28	..	..	8 49	..	10 25	..	11 45	2 13	2 40	..	..	5 5	5 57	..
TROWBRIDGE	dep.	7 11	8 35	9 6	10 30	11 3	11H25	12 40	2 30	2 34	3 0	3 54	4 9	5 23	6 15	..
BRADFORD-on-AVON	,,	7 22	8 15	8 45	9 15	10 44	..	11 45	12 50	2 44	3 10	..	4 18	5 33	6 26	..
BATH	arr.	7 46	8 40	9 10	9 39	11 8	11 24	12 9	1 14	3 8	3 24	4 14	4 42	5 48	6 52	..

WEEK-DAYS.   **SUNDAYS.**

		p.m.	p.m.	p.m.	p.m.		p.m.	p.m.			a.m.	p.m.	p.m.	p.m.		
MELKSHAM	dep.	..	6 20	6 20	8 43	..	9 17	..	..	..	9 15	..	..	7 7	..	
TROWBRIDGE	dep.	6 30	7 50	8 5	9 15	9 30	9 40	11 35	..	..	9 31	1 25	6 0	7 49	..	
BRADFORD-on-AVON	,,	6 41	..	8 15	9 27	9 40	9 48	11S43	..	..	9 40	1 36	6 9	8 0	..	
BATH	arr.	7 0	8 14	8 41	9 41	10 5			..	..	10 4	2 1	6 33	8 24	..	

A Not Mondays.   B Mondays only.   H Via Holt.   S Saturdays only.   W Wednesdays only.
Y Calls at Bradford to set down if required.

Paddington, July, 1906.   JAMES C. INGLIS, General Manager.

(10,000 Cr. 4to)   Arrowsmith, Printer, Quay Street, Bristol.   (B 503)

Handbill announcing reduced third-class fares following the reopening of Box Tunnel.

above the brick arches to prevent stone falls smashing them. Access doors are provided in the roof so that the space between the rock and tunnel arch can be inspected.

Today, shafts are sited at:

	Miles	Chains
No. 1	99	38
No. 2	99	60
No. 3	100	00
No. 4	100	18
No. 5	Closed 1910 by arch 20 ft above tunnel roof and shaft filled above arch	
No. 6	100	52

The diameter of the shafts is 25 ft and the deepest is 300 ft. As the height of the tunnel precludes inspection from the roof of a tunnel van, it was inspected by an engineer in a cradle slung from a 16-ton crane, a man perched on top of the jib shining a light on the roof. Nowadays the ceiling is reached by hoist, either jointed arm or scissor pattern.

A culvert cut from solid rock passed below the line 176 yd in from the eastern portal. It formerly had a roof of Barlow rails, but these were replaced by steel joists in 1928 at a cost of £205. For the annual inspection by the Bridge Department, a punt kept beside Corsham signal-box was placed on a manually propelled permanent-way trolley and pushed to the tunnel. Now an inflatable boat is used. Access is via Ministry of Defence property.

Today tunnel workers use battery-powered lamps but in times past two 40-gallon drums of parafin were trolleyed down from Corsham station to a hut near the eastern portal, where there was a storage tank holding over 80 gallons – enough for several months.

Tunnel ventilating shaft near Westwood, 25 June 1979.

(C.G. Maggs)

A view taken of the western portal of Box Tunnel, when repair to stonework was being undertaken, *c.* 1910.
Tunnel 'formers' can be seen on the far right. A spoil heap is to the left of the balustrade above the tunnel
mouth. The white board near the stone wagon in Pictor's siding reads 'Engines must not pass this board'.

(Author's Collection)

The tunnel is straight and the rising sun shines through on 6 and 7 April. For some
time these dates were queried, but were confirmed by BR engineers who made
observations in 1988. If there was no refraction the sun would shine through on Brunel's
birthday, 9 April, but Bessel's Refraction Tables were not readily available in England in
the 1830s. The earth's atmosphere causes a slight bend of the sun's rays which enables us
to see the sun rising 3 minutes before it is actually there, geometrically speaking, and
likewise we see it setting 3 minutes after it has gone.

Ears 'pop' when entering Box Tunnel as air is slightly compressed by the train because
the walls prevent it from being displaced outwards. This causes air on the outside of the
ear to be slightly denser than that on the inside. Moving the jaw equalises the pressure
more quickly. On leaving the tunnel ears 'pop' as the pressure slightly decreases.

The west front of the tunnel is superb. We should be thankful for the fact that the
Bristol Committee of the GWR was not so parsimonious as the London Committee and
allowed Brunel more scope for his flights of fancy. The massive cornice is set on
prominent curved stone corbels and surmounted by a moulded balustrade, while the
keystone is scroll-shaped and carved with an acanthus leaf. In 1986 this front was cleaned
and a viewing platform installed beside the A4. Until recently a permanent-way hut,
unusually built of stone, stood near the west portal. Today the spoil heaps are tree-
covered. An easily accessible one is on the north side of the west portal, and is
surmounted by a Second World War pillbox, its roof appropriately supported on rails.
No vent shafts are accessible to the public, as all are situated on private land.

Immediately west of the tunnel on the Up side was Pictor's stone siding, worked by a
ground frame electrically locked from Box and lifted on 4 October 1959. When a train
was required to work the siding, the signalman at Box communicated with his
counterpart at Corsham and advised him approximately how long the work would take.

Box, (Mill Lane) Halt, view Up, 23 May 1963.

(C.G. Maggs)

'Achilles' class 4–2–2 No. 3050 *Royal Sovereign* near the site of the later Mill Lane Halt.
It is working the 7.15 a.m. Falmouth–Paddington express, 23 September 1898.

(Author's Collection)

'Castle' class 4–6–0 No. 5082 *Swordfish* leaves Middle Hill Tunnel with the Up 'Bristolian', 27 March 1954.

(R.E. Toop)

57XX class 0–6–0PT No. 3759 (82B Bristol, St Philip's Marsh) leaving Middle Hill Tunnel with a Down pick-up freight, 28 June 1950.

(Pursey Short, courtesy Roger Venning)

4–6–0 No. 2920 *Saint David* passes Box signal-box, *c.* 1907, with a stopping train on a Temple Meads–Swindon running-in turn.

(Author's Collection)

The Appendix to the Working Time Table stated: 'When horses are pulling trucks over this Siding a chain must always be attached to the truck coupling, and the horses must not walk between the Siding and the Main Line. The men in charge are warned not to foul the Main Line in turning the horse or horses at any point.'

Beyond was Box (Mill Lane) Halt, opened on 31 March 1930 at an approximate cost of £800, and much closer to the centre of the village than Box station. The original timber platforms were later replaced by a 250 ft × 8 ft concrete structure surmounted by corrugated-iron shelters. As the platform held only four coaches, on longer trains passengers were required to travel in the rear four coaches. The 101¼ milepost was situated on the Up platform. Electric lighting was worked by a time switch. A leading porter was on duty 8.15 a.m. to 6 p.m. in a timber booking office to deal with passengers and parcels. Outside these hours it was treated like an unmanned halt, the guard collecting tickets and, if on the last train, extinguishing the lights in the days before the time switch was installed. The Box stationmaster visited every afternoon to collect the takings, which were then placed in a bag and kept in the safe at Box station overnight.

Receipts: Jan to Oct 1938   13,824 passgrs booked   £993 passgr receipts   £7 parcels
         "   "   1946   13,989   "   "   £1,409   "   "   £13   "

West of Box (Mill Lane) Halt a catch point was situated on the Up line. In 1945 a train carrying twelve Sherman tanks was proceeding through Box Tunnel when Guard Fred Payne sensed something was wrong. In the dark he was unable to see whether the train was going backwards or forwards, so he felt the wall with his shunting pole. Discovering it was running backwards, he leaped off, knowing his van would be derailed at the catch points and perhaps crushed.

Middle Hill Tunnel, 198 yd long, is cut through blue lias. Its portals are in Roman style, bearing the fasces symbol of authority based on a bunch of rods bound together. Only a short distance beyond the western portal was Box station, originally with timber buildings, but in about 1855 these were replaced by a Tudor-style structure, its hipped roof having a sloping end. The signal-box on the Up platform bore the interesting name-plate 'Box Signal Box'. When Col. Yolland inspected the mixed gauge in November 1875 he found the Up platform to be too narrow and required it to have a shelter, which was subsequently added.

Bath Electric Tramways motorbuses started a service from Bath to Box in September 1905, causing a monthly decrease of £21 (i.e. about an eighth of the takings) in GWR receipts for travel between these stations by December 1905. The GWR introduced a reduction in the rail fare from 10d return to 8d and thereby reduced the decrease to £7.

Some of the outgoing freight traffic from Box latterly consisted of tennis balls from Price's Rubber Works and small parcels despatched by the Westbourne Rubber Company, while inwards there was a coal depot on the Down side. Supplies for RAF Colerne also arrived, including bicycles for crews to reach the dispersal areas. The station closed to coal and freight from 3 June 1963.

In 1843 the staff consisted of a stationmaster, 1 booking-parcels clerk, 4 switchmen, 1 passenger porter, and 2 policemen for the level-crossing at Shockerwick. On 12 February 1921 the staff comprised: a stationmaster, 1 clerk, 1 goods clerk, 3 signalmen, 1 signalman-porter and 3 porters. The signalman-porter worked Farleigh Down box from 1 p.m. to 3 p.m. In 1960 there was a stationmaster, 3 signalmen, 2 porters, 1 junior clerk, 1 goods checker and 1 goods porter, though the latter was made redundant that year.

Box, view Up, *c.* 1900.
The engine shed is on the far left, with the stone wharf beyond.

(Author's Collection)

A 'Dean Goods' 0–6–0 at Box station, *c.* 1910.

(Paul De'Ath Collection)

A letter withdrawing passenger train services at Box.

(W. Talbot Collection)

YOUR REF.		BRITISH RAILWAYS	OUR REF.	FIN 27/22	B.R. 3/2
DATED		Western ...... REGION	DATE	11.12.1964	

TO Station Master,
BOX.

(Centre No.   )

FROM

Extn. 341

DIVISIONAL .... OFFICE,
ACCOUNTS SECTION.
HERBERT (Centre No.   )
BRISTOL

Withdrawal of Passenger Train Services from BOX and
BOX MILL LANE Stations on and from Monday 4th January 1965
- -

    In connection with the above I attach accountancy instructions for
your attention.

    Respecting outstandings it will probably be found expedient to
transfer these amounts by means of a Debit Transfer Voucher to Bath Spa,
thus leaving the outstandings on your final Account Current as 'NIL'.

                    for D.S.Hart.

BOX TRAFFIC 1960

		£
No. of passengers booked	12,917	1,528
Season tickets	451	333
	13,368	1,861
Parcels forwarded	7,496	3,024
〃 received	11,160	10
	13,368	3,034

GOODS TRAFFIC

	Number of Wagons	
	Forwarded	Received
Collection & Delivery	–	51
Other	–	100
General merchandise	131	480
Free-hauled (i.e. railway's own traffic)	82	140

In the 1960s cash was made up the previous day and forwarded to the Bristol cash office by the 7.35 a.m. Swindon to Bristol.

Half a mile beyond Box station, Ashley Cutting Crossing signal-box was open by 1884, and closed on 20 May 1905, when it was replaced by a footbridge.

Unloading 155-mm propellant charges at Farleigh Sidings, autumn 1943. The tramway trucks can be seen on the right and the entrance to the tunnel is beneath the canopy.

(Author's Collection)

A maze of crossovers remains on the ammunition tramway, Farleigh Sidings, 4 April 2002.
Behind the photographer the tramway descends to the tunnel.

(C.G. Maggs)

Farleigh Down siding, a mile west of Box, served a stone-loading dock at the foot of the mile-long counterbalanced tramway from Farleigh Down Quarry. The signal-box gave access to two looped sidings on the Down side, opened on 9 January 1882, and from 9 September 1910 on an 'as required' basis, but closed on 11 June 1930 when the private siding agreement terminated. The sidings and box reopened on 1 November 1937 when the quarry was purchased by the Air Ministry for storage, the first ammunition arriving on 1 May 1939. The GWR won the contract to lay sidings and the 1,000-ft-long platform complete with narrow-gauge track for the ammunition wagons. As the depot was a mile from the sidings, or 4 miles by lanes, a tunnel containing a conveyor belt was built from the main-line sidings to the depot. As this took a considerable time to construct, initially a 2,000-yd-long aerial ropeway was built. The cable was supported by 15-ft-high pylons set at 350 ft intervals and the system could handle a maximum of 60 tons an hour. Much of the ammunition brought back from Dunkirk in 1940 was sent to Farleigh Down Quarry.

The Cementation Company started excavation of the 2,200-yd-long tunnel in December 1938 but clay pressure caused the steel girders to buckle. The upper half of the tunnel – above the Kingsdown Road – was at a maximum depth of 180 ft, while the lower half set just below ground level was made by the 'cut and cover' method. The tunnel was on a constant gradient of 1 in 8½. Although the excavation was completed in the summer of 1940, lining took a further year. The tunnel ended at Farleigh sidings, 30 ft below the transfer platform. Narrow-gauge trucks were raised or lowered between the platform and conveyor belt by a Head-Wrightson tram creeper-retarder. Each link of a chain carried a projecting dog to engage a wagon axle and take it up or down the gradient. The belt first came into use in April 1942 and by that summer Farleigh Down Quarry contained 60,000 tons of ammunition, about half its capacity. When an air-raid warning was received, the brighter lighting was switched to blue to make it less visible from the air, though in practice many signalmen switched the lights off completely. Although the sidings were closed on 9 October 1950, the depot remained open until September 1963. The platform and creeper-retarder still remain today.

The signal-box at Farleigh Down was heated by a coal range, the engineer's gang delivering 15 cwt of coal annually, but with the box open continuously this proved insufficient. To renew the supply, the ploy was to wait for a light engine, unhitch the signal wire so that it was inoperable, stop the light engine to give a written order to pass the signal at danger, invite the driver into the box to have a cup of tea while the order was written, and then suggest he may wish to ask his fireman to throw some coal from the tender. About 10 cwt was usually decanted, the engine proceeded on its way and the wire was reconnected.

One resourceful signalman made a 20-ft-long rod to enable him to fish from Farleigh box. Unlike many others, the box was equipped with electric light and a kettle. During the Second World War, to enliven the twelve-hour shifts, one signalman purchased an electric radio, and drilled a hole in the floor to enable the lead to reach a socket in the locking room below. A crocodile clip attached the aerial to the telephone wires and the radio got marvellous reception!

Bathford Halt opened on 18 March 1929 at a cost of approximately £164. The 250 ft × 8 ft platforms, originally of timber and later of concrete, both had corrugated-iron shelters. Electric lights operated by time switches were added later. Set on an

Bathford Halt, view Up, 23 May 1963. The concrete components were manufactured in the depot at Taunton. The waiting shelters are of corrugated iron.

(C.G. Maggs)

The graceful bridge over the Avon at Bathford, 1846.

(Engraving by J.C. Bourne)

Bathampton, view Down, pre-1874, when it was converted to mixed gauge.
Note the crossbar signals and the transoms between the Up and Down roads.

(Author's Collection)

embankment, the platforms were slightly staggered. It displayed a relatively rare sign: 'Passengers are requested not to cross the line except under the bridge' – referring to the nearby road underbridge. The usual sign read 'over the bridge'. Tickets were issued by a GWR agent living in the farmhouse near the footpath to the Up platform. Guards collected tickets and handed them in to Box or Bathampton stations. Passengers were required to travel in the last four coaches. Beyond the halt a Bath stone semi-elliptical arch of 87 ft spans the Avon.

The double-track junction at Bathampton was altered 10 February 1986 so that for a short distance trains to Bradford-on-Avon travel on the Down main line.

The main stone building at Bathampton, opened in 1857, was on the Down platform, and both platforms were extended westwards in July 1898. Staff on 30 December 1920 consisted of a stationmaster, 3 signalmen, 3 porters and 1 district lampman. Around 1960 the stationmaster, 3 signalmen and 2 porters were reduced to 3 signalmen and a leading porter, the station being supervised from Box. The leading porter was responsible for morning bookings, parcels, station cleaning, checking wagons in the private siding and making freight rolling stock returns. The Box goods checker travelled with the 9.05 a.m. Chippenham to Bathampton freight to assist with shunting, protection of Glass's Crossing and recovery of ropes and sheets. Abolishing the post of Bathampton stationmaster saved annually:

	£
Class 3 salary	690
On call out of hours	50
National Health	26
Uniform	12
Annual leave	_34_
	812
Less difference of porter to leading porter	_48_
	764

TRAFFIC AT BATHAMPTON 1960

		£
Passengers	7,416	679
Parcels	362	19

GOODS RECEIVED

Coal and coke	97 tons
General merchandise	3,360 tons – totally timber for the private siding. Except for shunting, number-taking and collection of ropes and sheets, no work was involved.
Free-hauled (i.e. BR traffic)	
Forwarded	1,736 tons
Received	5,157 tons

The engineering department at Bathampton gave little work to station staff other than the collection of On Company's Service vouchers and the task of coupling wagons. Staff comprised five permanent-way and seven engineering department staff. They moved to Ashton Meadows, Bristol in the mid-1960s. Except on Thursdays, when he had to remain until 4.30 p.m. to keep the engineering department wages secure, the leading porter finished at 2 p.m. and for the rest of the day Bathampton became an unstaffed halt. Not more than £2 per week was taken in the period between 2 p.m. to 6 p.m. and this was mainly schoolchildren travelling from Bathampton to Bathford and the occasional passenger buying a cheap day ticket to Bath.

When the post of Bathampton stationmaster was combined with that of Box, because the train service was unsuitable for him travelling between the two, and there was no direct bus service, he was granted a mileage allowance for his car, but BR refused to refund the four daily bridge tolls required by his two visits. From 1 November 1964 the mileage allowance ranged from 5½d for a car up to 940 cc and 8d for 1801 cc and above. From 4 January 1965, when the local train service to Swindon was withdrawn, the station was reduced to an unstaffed halt. It closed completely on 3 October 1966, the closure date of a number of other stations on the Bathampton to Weymouth line.

Bathampton goods yard, situated on the inside curve of the Bradford-on-Avon line, closed 10 June 1963. Further south were J.T. Holmes & Company Ltd's two timber sidings, used from 25 August 1922 until 31 March 1965. There was also the siding used by the engineering department. When Messrs Harding & Son, printers, relocated to Batheaston from Bristol, they forwarded traffic from Bathampton from 4 December 1920. About 2 tons of paper were despatched daily in small consignments, mostly to stations in South Wales.

The signal-box at the Up end of the Down platform closed on 21 September 1956 and was replaced by a flat-roofed modern structure on the opposite side of the line. Due to the introduction of multiple aspect signalling, it had a short life and closed on 17 August 1970.

A Down broad-gauge express west of Bathampton, c. 1890. The engine is one of the last batch of 'Rover' class 4–2–2s with a flush-riveted smokebox. The train consists of narrow-bodied convertible coaches on broad-gauge underframes.

(Author's Collection)

No. 46004 emerges from the Up Loop, 10 May 1978.

(The Revd Alan Newman)

Hampton Row footbridge, view Up, 15 September 1983.

(John Mann)

A Down refuge siding was added in the 1880s to cater for additional traffic caused by the opening of the Severn Tunnel. Access was from the Down main line and it ran parallel with the Bradford-on-Avon branch, while the Up refuge siding, added at about the same time, was west of the station. It was extended and converted into an Up loop on 1 November 1942, when a Down loop was also brought into use on the opposite side of the line. Towards the western end of these loops was Bathampton West signal-box opened on 19 October 1942 and closed on 21 September 1956. The Down loop was taken out of use on 17 August 1970 but the Up loop remains. On one occasion a goods train was too long for the loop by two wagons, which meant that when the points were set for the Up main, these wagons were derailed by trap points. When the train in the refuge siding eventually moved forward, the derailed wagons ripped up the track.

Hampton Row Halt, adjacent to a level-crossing and serving a street of that name in an area not reached by road transport, opened on 18 March 1907, closed as a wartime economy measure on 25 April 1917, and was dismantled in 1920. The Kennet & Avon Canal here is above the railway; it had to be diverted south when the line was built and a ¾ mile-long high retaining wall with a pronounced batter constructed. It has been insensitively strengthened and partly replaced with brick.

The line continues through Sydney Gardens in an attractive manner, not spoiling and adding to their interest. James Tunstall, in his *Rambles in Bath & District* published in 1847, says that the railway and canal, 'so far from detracting from, are made to increase the beauty of the promenades'. This high quality is reflected in the many Grade II structures: the graceful 29 ft 6 in elliptical-arched Beckford Road bridge, and the Sydney Road bridge; the finely dressed retaining wall with its pronounced curved batter; the unusual balustraded stone wall on the other side of the line; and the two ornamental bridges of 30 ft span, one elliptical on the skew with a balustraded parapet and small side arch over a footpath, the other an attractive iron bridge with pierced spandrels and an iron balustrade.

Sydney Gardens, Bath, view Up, *c.* 1845.

(Engraving by Charles Davies)

No. 47284 leaves the Up Loop, Bathampton, with a weed-killing train, 17 May 1984.

(C.G. Maggs)

2–4–0 No. 14 west of Bathampton with an Up express, *c.* 1890. Built in May 1888, it was officially renewed as a 4–4–0 in 1894. Note the mixed-gauge main line, but that the Up Refuge Siding is only standard gauge.

(Author's Collection)

54XX class 0–6–0PT No. 5403 approaching Bathampton with the 1.18 p.m. Bath–Trowbridge,
25 July 1957. Note the water crane beside the first coach of the 'B' set.

(Russell Leitch)

72XX class 2–8–2T No. 7242 leaves the Up Loop with a mineral train, 28 September 1951.

(The Revd Alan Newman)

No. 7015 *Carn Brea Castle* passes Sydney Gardens on 31 March 1955
with the 3.35 p.m. Bristol Temple Meads–Swindon stopping train.

(The Revd Alan Newman)

As Bath station was in such a decrepit condition, a special platform was built in Sydney Gardens,
adjacent to the Up line, for the reception of Princess Helen on 13 June 1889.

(Author's Collection)

The west portal of Sydney Gardens West Tunnel, 15 September 1983.

(John Mann)

A temporary station was erected in Sydney Gardens. This came about because towards the end of the nineteenth century many complaints were received about the state of Bath station. So when Princess Helen made a visit on 13 June 1889, instead of her using the dilapidated structure, on arrival at Bath her train was drawn back on the Up line for half a mile to where a special temporary platform awaited in beautiful surroundings.

The line passes through the two Sydney Gardens tunnels: the East, 77 yd in length, and the West at 99 yd. Soon after emerging from the latter it crosses Pultency Road where its stone bridge was replaced by a steel span in 1974. The railway approaches Bath Spa over the thirty-one arches of the 255-yd-long Dolemeads Viaduct. The viaduct proved a useful escape route for dwellings flooded on 25 October 1882, a rescuer reporting: 'Those houses nearest the GWR were reached by long ladders from the parapet of the viaduct to the roofs. By removing tiles and breaking through the ceilings we reached some 50 imprisoned families.' Temporary accommodation for the flood victims was offered in the GWR waiting rooms, with food for the children provided by E.B. Titley, a Bath grocer, and his friends.

In 1854 the vicar of St Matthew's, Widcombe, was concerned that there was no infants' school in the Dolemeads. Land was purchased from the GWR at a cost of £350 and a school built in 1855, partly under and partly against archway No. 14 of the viaduct, and adjacent to No. 15, which is today's Broadway. Arch No. 14, with an extension, measured 58 ft × 26½ ft, was lined with ashlar, and below the arch was covered with Croggan's patent asphalt felt. There was a smaller room in arch No. 12. The school was heated by stoves. Arch No. 11 and the adjoining land formed a dry and spacious playground with flower borders and a swing. In 1900 a new school was built and the old school used as a mission room. The arches have recently been bricked to about three-quarters of their height and windows placed at the top to create lock-ups known as Ferry Court.

Widcombe Infants' School, 1855, partly situated under Dolemeads Viaduct.

(Author's Collection)

Immediately beyond Dolemeads Viaduct is St James's Bridge, which has a wide arch and two side arches all carrying water, with the footpath cantilevered out over the river.

Bath Spa, Grade II listed, is placed in a cramped situation between two river bridges set only 700 ft apart. Into this space, in addition to passenger facilities, was originally squeezed an engine shed and goods depot, the latter set at right angles to the main line and access being by wagon turntable. When Col. Yolland inspected the completed mixed gauge between Bristol and Swindon in November 1875 he commented that Bath station was not good for goods or passengers, and at the latter station he found rows of pillars only 3 ft 2 in from the platform edges.

The station buildings are situated on both sides of a twenty-arch viaduct. The architectural style is debased Elizabethan, with Gothic windows and Romanesque ornamentation. The north front, facing the city, is of asymmetrical design with three Jacobean-style gables and a central oriel window. The building was flanked by curved wing walls forming a carriage sweep. In 1845 an eastern wing was built containing, among other things, a first-class waiting room. A canopy above the entrance allowed carriage passengers to alight in the dry. Attractive radial fanlights are set above the doorways.

The building adjacent to the Down platform is much plainer in style but it, too, had an exterior canopy to shelter carriage passengers. Until 1897 the two platforms and the four roads between were covered by a train shed. Of 40 ft span, it was supported at the sides by twenty-six large iron columns placed so near the platform edge that there was little room for movement when coach doors were open. As the trains are at first-floor level, in order to avoid an outward thrust on the walls built on arches, Brunel designed the roof timbers like long arms of cranes which met in the centre, short arms being held down by the side walls at the rear of the platforms.

Bath station from Beechen Cliff, *c.* 1893. The Down platform has been extended beyond the train shed
and a building and canopy can be seen to its left. At the Down platform is a Dean-style tender engine,
and the rear of the train has a 40-ft passenger luggage van and a long clerestory compo, or slip, coach.

(Author's Collection)

No. 4073 *Caerphilly Castle*, now preserved in the Steam Museum of the Great Western Railway,
heads a Paddington–Temple Meads train into Bath, 19 March 1955.

(The Revd Alan Newman)

The GWR section of the Bath St John's Ambulance Brigade, 1904.

(Author's Collection)

The interior of Bath train shed, *c.* 1846.

(Engraving by J.C. Bourne)

Feelings about the condition of the station were so strong that on 2 April 1889 the town clerk submitted a memorial to the directors signed by 1,100 citizens. It pointed out that except for lengthening the Down platform to 400 ft, and the Up to 270 ft in about 1880, the station was as originally built; the presence of pillars near the platform edge was dangerous; a carriage approach to platform level was required; and the staircase was narrow and exceedingly steep − objectionable anywhere, but intolerable at Bath, a resort for invalids. Eventually on 14 February 1895 shareholders agreed that £15,000 be spent on station improvements which were 'in hand'. The work had begun on 23 March, when platelayers slewed the Up line 6 ft towards the Down, allowing carpenters to lay 3,600 ft of planking to widen the platform and give 8 to 9 ft between the platform edge and the obstructive columns. A few weeks later the Down side was similarly treated. The station was electrically lit and must have been one of the first in the country to have this form of illumination. At first the GWR generated its own power at Bath, but in 1902 purchased a supply from Bath Corporation at 1½d a unit, a price the GWR considered low enough to abolish its own installation. In 1897 the overall roof was removed, despite a letter to the *Bath Chronicle* pleading for the retention of the 'fine train shed'. An Up bay platform holding four coaches was added, and the main platforms lengthened as far as possible without blocking access to the stub sidings at the end of both platforms. Wagons were placed on these sidings by a shunting horse, a wagon turntable directing them to the desired line.

Following the Bath blitz of April 1942 the damage to the canopy cost £2,577 to repair. The stub sidings were removed in January 1960, which allowed the platforms to be lengthened, the Down from eight to ten coaches and the Up from nine to fifteen. It was ironic that soon after the platforms were extended trains became shorter and the full length of the Up platform is rarely used today. Each platform was served by two hydraulic lifts, one for passengers and the other for luggage. An employee on the platform who wanted to raise the luggage lift called as a warning 'Below!' before pulling the operating handle. As an economy measure on 30 March 1925 the passenger lifts were closed to general passengers, although retained for the disabled, thereby releasing three collectors for other duties. In 1965–6 the four hydraulic lifts were removed, as they were unnecessary since road access had been built. The pump station near the Up end of the Down platform was demolished, as were the cottages occupied by the permanent-way inspector and the bridge inspector who also dealt with the Severn Tunnel.

From 1845 until 26 January 1936 an open girder footbridge offered a direct connection between the Up platform and the Royal Hotel, built by Chadwick the railway contractor, on the opposite side of the street.

SPEED LIMITS 2002

	mph
East of Swindon	125
Through Swindon station	85
Swindon West to 103¼ milepost	125
103¼–105½	100
105½–106 miles 62 chains	75
Through Bath station	40
107 miles 2 chains–108¼ milepost	90

Chapter Four

PASSENGER TRAIN SERVICES

In 1837 coaches took at least ten hours for the journey from London to Bath, at a cost of £1 15s inside, plus 6s in tips and 10s for refreshment, though an outside seat reduced the fare to 15s. The less affluent travelled by stage wagon at about 4 mph and a fare of 9s, and slept on straw in stable lofts. The opening of the GWR brought Bath within about four hours of London and offered fares of £1 7s 6d first class, 19s 6d second and 11s 6d third.

With the extension of the GWR from Faringdon Road to Wootton Bassett Road, eight trains ran each way on weekdays to and from Paddington, with three on Sundays. The same service continued when the line was extended through to Chippenham on 31 May 1841. With the opening to Bath on 30 June 1841, seven trains were provided each way from Paddington to Bath and Bristol, plus one from Cirencester to Bristol. Most took about 65 minutes for the 29½ miles from Swindon to Bath, though one running non-stop covered the distance in an hour. On Sundays three ran each way from Paddington and one from Cirencester. An interesting note on early timetables read: 'London time is kept at all stations on the railway, which is about 4 minutes earlier than Reading time; 5½ minutes before Steventon time; 8 minutes before Chippenham time; 11 minutes before Bath and Bristol time; and 14 minutes before Bridgwater time.' It was the coming of the railway which induced people to adopt Greenwich time as standard.

On 19 July 1843 Prince Albert travelled to Bristol to launch the SS *Great Britain*. The centre of the Down platform at Bath was fitted up as a drawing room and the floor covered with a crimson cloth, where the mayor, town clerk and a deputation of inhabitants presented him with an address. Temporary tiered staging was erected on the Up platform and tickets sold to spectators. So that they could have a good view, the train reversed after the prince got out. The four-coach royal train was headed by 'Fire Fly' class 2–2–2 *Damon*, built in March 1842 and one of the longest-lived of its class, not being withdrawn until July 1870. It was driven by Daniel Gooch and made an average speed of 46 mph between Paddington and Bath.

The first train in the world exclusively for the post office started running between Paddington and Bristol on 1 February 1855. Comprising two sorting carriages and a van, its average speed, including seven stops, was 31.7 mph. Fourteen years later a first-class coach was added, the post office insisting that this be the limit. In 1875 the GWR introduced a newspaper train for the West Country which left Paddington at 5.30 a.m.

Although the Severn Tunnel was opened in 1886 it was not until early 1887 that Paddington to South Wales trains were diverted via Chippenham, Bristol and the Severn Tunnel, instead of around by Gloucester. Express trains of that period consisted of about six coaches, each weighing approximately 25 tons. Although carried on eight wheels, they were not on bogies, the inside axles being rigid but with side play on the outer axles.

The timetable for January to April 1902 showed eighteen Down trains between Swindon and Bath, expresses taking about 38 minutes and stopping trains 1 hour

GREAT WESTERN RAILWAY

LONDON TO BRISTOL.

ON and after WEDNESDAY NEXT, the 16th of DECEMBER, 1840, the Line will be FURTHER EXTENDED to the WOOTTON BASSET ROAD STATION (80 Miles from London), for the Conveyance of Passengers, Carriages, Horses, Goods, and Parcels. The SHRIVENHAM STATION will also be OPENED.

HOURS OF DEPARTURE DAILY (EXCEPTING SUNDAYS).

DOWN FROM PADDINGTON TO		Departure from Paddington	UP TO PADDINGTON FROM	
		H. M.		H. M.
Wootton Basset Road	A.M.	8 0	Wootton Basset Road ... A.M. *(Mail Train.)*	2 30
Maidenhead		8 30	Reading	7 30
Wootton Basset Road		10 0	Slough	9 0
Slough		10 30	Maidenhead	9 50
Wootton Basset Road		12 0	Wootton Basset Road	8 30
Slough	P.M.	1 30	Reading	11 0
Wootton Basset Road		2 0	Wootton Basset Road	10 15
Wootton Basset Road		4 0	Wootton Basset Road	11 30
Slough		4 30	Slough	8 0
Reading		5 0	Wootton Basset Road P.M.	1 15
Maidenhead		6 0	Wootton Basset Road	2 30
Wootton Basset Road		7 0	Slough	6 0
Reading		8 0	Wootton Basset Road	4 30
Wootton Basset Road		8 53	Maidenhead	7 45
(Mail Train.)			Wootton Basset Road	6 30

SUNDAY DOWN TRAINS.

		H. M.
Wootton Basset Road	A.M.	8 0
Slough		8 30
Reading		9 0
Slough		9 30
Wootton Basset Road	P.M.	2 0
Reading		5 0
Slough		7 0
Wootton Basset Road		8 53
(Mail Train.)		

SUNDAY UP TRAINS.

		H. M.
Wootton Basset Road	A.M.	2 30
(Mail Train.)		
Reading		7 30
Slough		9 0
Wootton Basset Road	P.M.	2 0
Slough		4 0
Wootton Basset Road		6 30
Reading		5 0
		8 0

BRISTOL AND BATH.

Horses, Carriages, &c.. will be conveyed by Railway between BRISTOL and BATH STATIONS on and after the 16th of DECEMBER. The SALTFORD and TWERTON STATIONS will also be OPENED for the Conveyance of PASSENGERS, PARCELS, &c.

HOURS of DEPARTURE, Regulated by BRISTOL TIME, until the whole Line shall be Opened. DAILY (excepting Sundays).

Train Bills and further particulars may be had at the Railway Offices and Stations on TUESDAY, the 15th Instant. By Order of the Directors,

11th December, 1840. CHAS. A. SAUNDERS, } Secretaries. THOMAS OSLER. }

Timetable for 16 December 1840, when the line was extended to Wootton Bassett Road.

Great Western Railway.

LONDON to CIRENCESTER, BATH, BRISTOL, and BRIDGEWATER, on and after the 30th June, 1841.

BRIDGEWATER is 11 miles from TAUNTON, 42 miles from EXETER, and 90 miles from Plymouth; CIRENCESTER is 15 miles from CHELTENHAM, 12 miles from STROUD, and 17 miles from GLOUCESTER.

HORSES and CARRIAGES being at those Stations, which are distinguished by Capital Letters, ten minutes before the time specified for the departure of a Train, will be conveyed on this Railway.——POST HORSES are kept in readiness at the Principal Stations.
Notice may be given at Bristol Station for Carriages to be brought from Clifton, or the neighbourhood to the Station, at a charge of 8s. 6d. including the Post Boy.

TIME TABLE.

LONDON TIME is kept at all the stations on the Railway, which is about 4 minutes earlier than READING time; 5½ minutes before STEVENTON time; 8 minutes before CHIPPENHAM time; 11 minutes before BATH and BRISTOL time; and 14 minutes before BRIDGEWATER time.

DAILY, EXCEPTING SUNDAYS.

Distance from Paddington.	Down Trains.	a. m. 8 0 From Bristol to Bridgewater.	a. m. 9 0 From Bath to Bristol, and Bridgewater.	a. m. 8 45 From Cirencester & Swindon, to Bath & Bristol; 11 30 From Bristol to Bridge-water.	a. m. 8. 0 From Paddington to Cirencester, Bath, Bristol, and Bridgewater.	a. m. 12.30 From Bath to Bristol.	a. m. 10. 0 From Paddington and Cirencester, Bath, Bristol, and Bridgewater	a. m. 11. 0 From Paddington to Cirencester, Bath, Bristol, and Bridgewater.	noon. 12. 0 From Paddington to Cirencester, Bath, Bristol, and Bridgewater.	p. m. 5. 0 From Bath to Bristol.	p. m. 2. 0 From Paddington Cirencester, to Bath and Bristol; 7 0 From Bristol to Bwater.	p. m. 7.30 From Bath to Bristol.	p. m. 5. 0 From Paddington to Cirencester, Bath, and Bristol.	p. m. 10. 0 From Bath to Bristol.	Mail. p. m. 8.55 From Paddington to Cirencester, Bath, and Bristol.	Every Day GOODS. a. m. 4.30 From Paddington to Cirencester, Bath and Bristol; 7 a.m. From Bristol to Bwater.	Every Day GOODS. p. m. 9.30 From Paddington to Cirencester, Bath and Bristol; 8 a.m. From Bristol to Bwater.
Miles.	*Starting from*	h. m.	h. m.	h. m.	h. m.	h. m.	h. m.	h. m.	h. m.	h. m.	h. m.	h. m.	h. m.	h. m.	h. m.	h. m.	h. m.
	PADDINGTON				8. 0		10. 0	11. 0	12. 0		2. 0		5. 0		8.55	4.30	9.30
	and Starting from CIRENCESTER			7 50				12.50			3.50				11.30		
77	*Calls at* SWINDON JUNCTION			8.45	10.40		12.35	1.45	2.50		4.45		7.40			9.10	2.15
82¼	WOOTON BASSETT			8.55				2. 5			5. 5		8. 0		12.10	11.15	3. 0
93¾	CHIPPENHAM			9.20	11. 0			2.30	3.35		5.30		8.25			12. 0	3.45
98¾	Corsham			9.30	11.20			2.40					8.35				
101¾	Box			9.38	11.30			2.48			5.45				8.55		
106¾	BATH		9. 0	9.50	11.45	12.30	1.35	3. 0	4. 0	5. 0	5.55	7.30	8.50	10. 0	12.40	12.45	9.45
108	Twerton			9.55						5. 5				10. 5			
110¾	Saltford		9.13			12.42				5.13							
113½	Keynsham		9.20	10.10		12.48		3.15		5.20		7.48		10.18			
118	BRISTOL Arrival		9.30	10.20	12.10	12.58	2. 0	3.25	4.30	5.30	6.20	7.58	9.15	10.26	1. 5	1.30	6. 0
...	BRISTOL Departure	8. 0	9.45	11.30	12.20		2.10		4.40		7. 0				1.15	7 p.m.	8 a.m.
126	Nailsea	8.18	10. 5						4.58		7.18					7.18	8.18
129¼	CLEVEDON ROAD at Yatton	8.28	10.15	11.57	12.45				5. 8		7.28					7.28	8.28
133¼	Banwell	8.35		12. 5							7.35					7.35	8.35
134½	WESTON-SUPER-MARE Junction	8.42	10.35	12.15			2.45		5.20		7.42					7.42	8.42
144¼	HIGHBRIDGE	9.10	10.58	12.38	1.15				5.36		8.10					8.10	9.10
151	BRIDGEWATER	9.30	11.10	12.50	1.35		3.20		5.40		8.30				2.25	8.30	9.30

Distance from Bridgwater	Up Trains.	a.m. 7.0 From Bristol to Bath, Cirencester, and London.	a.m. 8. 0 From Bristol to Bath.	a.m. 8. 0 From Bridg. to Bristol; 10.0 From Bristol to Bath.	a.m. 11. 0 From Bristol to Bath.	a.m. 10. 0 From Bridg. to Bristol; 12. 0 From Bristol to Bath and London.	a.m. 11.30 From Bridgewater to Bristol, Bath, Cirencester, and London.	p.m. 1.30 From Bridgewater to Bristol, Bath, Cirencester, and London.	p.m. 4. 0 From Bristol to Bath.	p.m. 3.30 From Bridgewater to Bristol, Bath, and London.	p.m. 6. 0 From Bristol to Bath, Swindon, and Cirencester	p.m. 5. 0 From Bridgewater to Bristol, and Bath.	p.m. 7. 0 From Bridg. to Bristol; 9. 0 From Bristol to Bath	Mail p.m. 11.40 From Bridgewater to Bristol, Bath, and London.	Goods every Day a.m. 8. 0 From Bridgr. to Bristol; 3.15 From Bristol to Bath, and London.	Goods every Day p.m. 7. 0 From Bridgr. to Bristol; 9.30 From Bristol to Bath, and [illegible]
Miles.	*Starting from*	h.m.	h.m.	h.m.	h.m.	h.m.	h.m.	h.m.	h.m.	h.m.	h.m.	h.m.	h.m.	h.m.	h.m.	h.m.
	BRIDGEWATER			8. 0		10. 0	11.30	1.30		3.30		5. 0	7. 0	11.40	8. 0	7. 0
6¼	*Calling at* HIGHBRIDGE			8.14		10.14		1.44		3.44		5.14	7.15		8.14	7.15
16¼	WESTON-SUPER-MARE Station			8.20		10.20	11.50	1.50				5.20	7.20		8.20	7.20
17¾	Banwell			8.42						4 12		5.45				
21¾	CLEVEDON ROAD at Yatton			8.50		10.50	12.20			4.20		5.55	7.55		8.50	7.55
[illegible]	Nailsea			9. 0		10.58		2.22				6. 5	8. 5		9. 0	8. 5
[illegible]	BRISTOL Arrival			9.20		11.16	12.50	2.50		4.50		6.30	8.30	12.50	9.20	8.30
	BRISTOL Depar.	7.0	8.0	10. 0	11. 0	12. 0	1. 0	3. 0	4. 0	5. 0	6. 0	6.50	9. 0	1. 0	3.15	9.30
37¾	Keynsham		8.10		11.10			3.10	4.10		6.10	7. 0	9.10			
40¾	Saltford		8.15			12.15			4.15		6.15		9.15			
43	Twerton		8.22		11.20				4.22			7.12				
44¾	BATH	7.25	8.28	10.20	11.26	12.25	1.20	3.25	4.28	5.25	6.30	7.20	9.26	1.20	4. 0	10.30
49¼	Box	7.40				12.40				5.40	6.45					
52¼	Corsham	7.55				12.55					7. 0					
57¼	CHIPPENHAM	8. 5		10.50		1. 5	1.50			6. 0	7.10			1.50	4.50	11.20
68¼	WOOTON BASSETT	8.30				1.30				6.23	7.35				5.45	12-10
74	SWINDON JUNCTION	8.38		11.25		1.40	2.25	4.40		6.33	7.45			2.25	7. 0	3. 0
92	CIRENCESTER Arrival	9.35					3.35	5.30			8.25					
151	PADDINGTON Arrival	11.20		2.10		4.30	5. 0	7.20		9.10				5.20	12. 0	8. 0

ON SUNDAYS.

Down Trains.	a. m. 8. 50 From Bath to Bristol and Bridgewater.	a. m. 8. 45 From Swindon to Bath and Bristol.	a. m. 9. 0 From London to Cirencester, Bath, Bristol and Bridgewater.	p. m. 3. 30 From Bath to Bristol.	p. m. 2. 0 From London to Cirencester, Bath, Bristol, and Bridgewater.	p. m. 9. 30 From Bath to Bristol.	Mail. 8. 55 From London to Cirencester, Bath, Bristol, and Bridgewater.
Starting from PADDINGTON			9. 0		2. 0		8.55
Calling at SWINDON JUNCTION		8.45	11.50		4.51		11.30
CIRENCESTER			12.50		5.40		
WOTTON BASSETT		8.55	12.15		5.10		12.10
CHIPPENHAM		9.20	12.40		5.35		
Corsham		9.30	12.50		5.45		
Box		9.38	1. 0		5.53		
BATH	8.50	9.50	1.10	3.30	6. 5	9.30	12.40
Twerton		9.55	1.20	3.34		9.34	
Saltford	9. 3		1.28	3.42		9.42	
Keynsham	9.10	10.10	1.32	3.48	6.25	9.48	
BRISTOL Arrival	9.20	10.20	1.40	4. 0	6.35	10. 0	1. 5
BRISTOL Departure	9.30		1.50		7. 0		1.15
Nailsea	9.46		2.10		7.18		
CLEVEDON ROAD at Yatton	9.54		2.18		7.28		
Banwell	10. 2				7.35		
WESTON-SUPER-MARE	10.10		2.30		7.42		
Highbridge	10.30		2.48		8.10		
BRIDGEWATER	10.45		3. 0		8.30		2.25

Up Trains.	a.m. 8. 0 From Bristol to Bath.	a.m. 8. 0 From Bridgw. to Bristol; 10 0 From Bridgw. to Bath Cirencester and London	a.m. 2.30 From Bristol to Bath.	p.m. 2. 0 From Bridgewater to Bath, Bristol, Cirencester and London.	p.m. 6. 0 From Bristol to Bath and Cirencester.	p.m. 7. 0 From Bridgewater to Bristol and Bath.	MAIL. 11.30 From Bridgewater to Bristol, Bath, and London.
Starting from BRIDGEWATER		8. 0		2. 0		7. 0	11.40
Calling at HIGHBRIDGE		8.14		2.20		7.15	
WESTON-SUPER-MARE (Station.)		8.20		2.40		7.20	
Banwell		8.42				7.48	
CLEVEDON ROAD, at Yatton		8.50		2.50		7.56	
Nailsea		9. 0		3. 0		8. 5	
BRISTOL ARRIVAL		9.20		3.20		8.30	12.50
BRISTOL DEPARTURE	8. 0	10. 0	2.30	3.30	6. 0	8.40	1. 0
Keynsham	8.10	10.10	2.40		6.10	8.50	
Saltford	8.15		2.45		6.15		
Twerton	8.23		2.53			9. 5	
BATH	8.30	10.25	3. 0	3.55	6.30	9.15	1.20
Box		10.40			6.45		
Corsham		10.55		4.25	7. 0		
CHIPPENHAM		11. 5		4.35	7.10		1.50
WOOTON BASSETT				5. 0	7.35		
SWINDON JUNCTION		11 45		5.10	7.45		
CIRENCESTER		12.50					2.25
LONDON		2.45		8. 0			5.20

Passengers, Parcels, &c. from Bridgewater, Bristol, Bath, and Chippenham, proceeding to Gloucester, Cheltenham, &c., may be booked by the UP TRAINS to "SWINDON JUNCTION," proceeding by the DOWN TRAINS to Cirencester, where Conveyances are in waiting to forward Passengers. In like manner, Passengers from Gloucestershire, &c., can proceed "WEST" by coming to the "SWINDON JUNCTION," and thence by the DOWN TRAINS to Chippenham, Bath, Bristol, and Bridgewater. The GOODS TRAIN PASSENGERS will be conveyed in uncovered Trucks by the Goods' Trains only, and 14-lbs. of Luggage allowed for each.

COACHES will run from Bridgewater to Exeter, Plymouth, Devonport, Barnstaple, and other Towns in the West of England, and from Cirencester to Cheltenham, Gloucester, &c.
OMNIBUSES, &c., will be at the Bristol, Bath, and Bridgewater Stations, for the Conveyance of Passengers on the arrival of each Train.
PARCELS may be Booked at the Railway Stations for all parts of the West of England, Gloucestershire, and Wales, and the Towns and Villages on each side of the Line of Railway.
FOUR DAILY DELIVERIES will be made in London, Cirencester, Bath, Bristol, and Bridgewater.
Separate Bills are published by the Company specifying the Rates of Charge for Goods, Cattle, &c., which may be obtained at any of the Stations.

[☞ TURN OVER.]

Timetable, 30 June 1841.

2 GREAT WESTERN.—Open to Exeter.

Miles	Down Trains.	4½	7½	6	11	8	9	10½	11	12	1½	2	4	5	5½	6½	7½	mail. 855	GOODS. 4½	9½	
	Trains leave	a.m	a.m.	a.m.	a.m.	a.m.	a.m.	a.m.	a.m.	noon	p.m.	p.m.	p.m.	p.m.	p.m.	p.m.	p.m.	p.m.	a.m.	p.m.	..
	PADDINGTON	..		6 0	..	8 0	9 0	10*15	11 0	12 0	1 30	2*0	4 0	5 0	5 30	6 30	7 30	8*55	4 30	9 30	..
5¾	Ealing	..	Mail to Exeter.	..	..	..	9 11	Mail to Bristol.	11 11	..	1 41	..	4 13	..	5 41	6 41	7 43	..	..	..	..
7¼	Hanwell	..		..	..	..	9 15		11 16	..	1 45	..	4 19	..	5 46	6 45	7 49	..	..	..	..
9	Southall	..		W	..	..	9 20		11 20	..	1 50	..	4 24	..	5 50	6 50	7 54	..	W	..	..
13	West Drayton	..		..	..	S	9 29		11 29	..	1 59	..	4 33	..	6 0	6 59	8 3	9 20	5 24	..	..
18	SLOUGH	..		6 35	..	8 25	9 45	10 55	11 45	12 38	2 16	2 38	4 46	5 38	6 12	7 15	8 16	9 30	5 44	10 30	..
22½	MAIDENHEAD	..		6 45	..	8 40	9 56	11 3	11 55	..		2 50	4 56	..	6 30		8 26	9 42	6 0	..	..
30¾	TWYFORD	..		..	..	9 5		..		1 8	..	3 8	5 12	6 3		..	8 42	..	..	11 14	..
35¾	READING	..	..	7 10	..	9 18	..	11 25	..	1 20	..	3 22	5 25	6 17	..	..	8 55	10 10	7 20	11 40	..
41½	PANGBOURNE	..	..	..	..	9 32	..	..	..	1 37	..	S		6 30	..	..	9 10	..	7 40	..	..
44¼	Goring	..	..	7 28	..	..	..	..	..	1 47	..	..	..	S	..	..	9 18	..	..	..	..
47¾	WALLINGFORD ROAD	..	..	..	..	9 46	..	11 58	..	..	..	3 45	..	6 45	..	..	9 27	10 35	..	12 20	..
53	DIDCOT (Junction)	..	..	7 44	..	9 58	11 15	12 12	..	2 6	..	3 58	..	6 58	..	..	9 40	10 48	8 20	12 45	..
55	APPLEFORD	..		..	..	10 10	..	..	..	2 14	..	..	..	..	..	..	9 50	..	10 10	..	..
56	ABINGDON ROAD	..	..	7 55	..	10 13	..	12 23	..	2 17	..	4 10	..	7 10	..	..	9 55	11 0	10 13	..	..
63	OXFORD	..	..	8 10	..	10 30	11 36	12 38	..	2 35	..	4 25	..	7 25	..	..	10 10	11 16	10 30	..	..
56¼	STEVENTON	..	..	7 50	..	..	..	..	..	2 17	..	..	..	7 8	..	..	..	..	..	..	..
63½	FARRINGDON ROAD	..	..	8 7	..	..	..	12 28	..	2 32	..	4 23	..	7 23	..	..	..	11 12	..	1 19	..
71½	SHRIVENHAM	..	..	..	..	10 40	..	..	..	2 50	..	4 41	..	7 40	..	..	..	..	9 30	..	..
77	SWINDON (Junction)	..	..	8 40	..	10 55	..	1 5	..	3 5	..	4 55	..	7 50	..	..	..	11 40	10 0	2 15	..
	CHELTENHAM (Departs for)	..	..	9 2	..	11 7	..	1 17	..	3 17	..	5 7	..	8 2	..	..	..	11 52	11 7	9 2	..
81½	Purton	..	..	9 10	..	..	..	1 27	..	..	..	5 17	..	..	..	..	..	..	..	9 10	..
85½	MINETY	..	..	9 20	..	11 23	..	1 33	..	3 33	..	5 27	..	8 22	..	..	..	..	11 23	9 20	..
96	CIRENCESTER	..	..	9 50	..	11 50	..	2 5	..	4 5	..	5 53	..	8 50	..	..	..	12 35	11 50	9 50	..
—	SWINDON Junction (Departs)	Passengers and Goods	..	8 50	..	11 5	..	1 15	..	3 15	..	5 5	..	8 0	..	..	..	11 50	11 10	2 30	..
82¾	WOOTTON BASSET		..	9 3	..	..	..	..	..	3 27	..	5 18	..	8 12	..	..	..	..	11 40	..	..
93¾	CHIPPENHAM		..	9 28	..	11 35	..	1 45	..	3 50	..	5 40	..	8 33	..	..	..	12 20	12 30	3 45	..
98¼	Corsham		..	9 38	..	11 47	..	..	..	4 2	..	..	..	8 48	..	..	..	..	..	..	..
101¼	Box		..	9 48	a.m.	11 57	p.m.	..	..	..	p.m.	6 0	..	8 52	..	p.m.	..	..	..	..	..
106¾	BATH	4 30	*7 15	10 0	11 0	12 10	1 0	2 10	..	4 20	5 30	6 15	..	9 10	..	9*30	..	12 50	1 10	4 30	..
108¼	Twerton	..	7 20	..	11 5	..	1 5	..	..	..	5 35	..	..	..	..	9 35	..	..	..	..	..
111¼	Saltford	..	7 28	..	11 13	..	1 12	..	..	..	5 45	..	..	..	..	9 42	..	..	..	..	..
113¾	Keynsham	..	7 35	10 20	11 20	..	1 20	..	..	4 35	5 50	..	..	..	..	9 49	..	..	..	..	..
118¼	BRISTOL arrival	5 20	7 45	10 30	11 30	12 35	1 30	2 36	..	4 50	6 0	6 40	..	9 40	..	10 0	..	1 15	1 45	6 20 a.m.	..
	BRISTOL departure	..	8 0	10 50	..	12 50	..	2 45	..	5 5	..	9 55	..	..	..	..	..	1 25	..	7 0	..
126¼	Nailsea	..	8 18	..	..	1 8	..	..	..	5 23	..	7 13	..	..	..	..	..	..	..	..	..
130¼	CLEVEDON ROAD, Yatton Junc.	..	8 28	11 18	..	1 18	..	3 8	..	5 34	..	7 23	..	..	..	..	..	..	..	7 45	..
133¾	Banwell	..	..	11 25	..	..	..	..	..	5 43	..	..	..	..	..	..	..	..	..	7 58	..
136¾	WESTON SUPER MARE	..	8 45	11 35	..	1 28	..	3 23	..	5 50	..	7 40	..	..	..	..	..	..	..	8 10	..
145¼	HIGHBRIDGE, near Burnham	..	9 3	11 53	..	..	..	3 41	..	6 10	..	7 58	..	..	..	..	..	..	..	8 42	..
151½	BRIDGEWATER	a.m	9 20	12 10	..	2 0	..	3 55	..	6 25	..	8 15	..	..	..	..	..	2 35	..	9 5	..
163	TAUNTON	8* 0	9 40	12 30	..	2 25	..	4 15	..	6 50	..	8 35	..	..	..	..	..	3 0	..	10 10	..
170	WELLINGTON	8 15	9 55	12 45	..	..	..	4 30	..	7 5	..	8 50	..	..	..	..	..	3 15	..	10 35	..
179	TIVERTON ROAD	8 34	10 15	1 10	..	2 55	..	4 50	..	7 30	..	9 15	..	..	..	..	..	3 35	..	11 30	..
181½	COLLUMPTON	8 39	10 20	1 17	..	3 0	..	..	..	7 37	..	9 22	..	..	..	..	..	3 40	..	11 40	..
185¼	Hele	8 49	10 28	1 27	..	3 10	..	5 3	..	7 47	..	9 33	..	..	..	..	..	..	..	12 0	..
193¾	EXETER	9 0	10 45	1 45	..	3 30	..	5 20	..	8 5	..	9 50	..	..	..	..	..	4 5	..	12 30	..

Timetable, May 1844.

10 minutes. Only fourteen trains ran from Bath to Swindon, expresses taking about 45 minutes and stopping trains 1 hour 25 minutes. Competition arrived in September 1905 when Bath Electric Tramways Company started running motorbuses to Box and Corsham.

The July 1938 timetable recorded seventeen Down trains, expresses taking about 37 minutes and stopping trains 1 hour, while in the Up direction twelve ran, expresses taking about 41 minutes and stopping trains 1 hour. Stopping trains between Bath and Swindon were withdrawn on 4 January 1965, when all intermediate stations except Bathampton and Chippenham were closed.

The Paddington to Bristol Temple Meads HST service was launched on 4 October 1976 and by the 1980s long-distance commuting was common, as people realised that they could travel daily to London by HST from Bath and Chippenham in less time and in more comfort than making a shorter journey originating nearer London. On 29 September 2002 the timetable was recast so that Temple Meads to Paddington services call at Bath at 23 and 53 minutes past each hour and Chippenham 5 and 35 minutes past the hour. The 15.10 Temple Meads to Paddington and the 17.15 return was worked from that date by a ten-car Adelante providing about a hundred additional seats over an HST's capacity. The fastest train to Paddington takes 1 hour 9 minutes from Chippenham and 1 hour 22 minutes from Bath, with Down times being 1 hour 8 minutes and 1 hour 21 minutes respectively. From 21 June 1998 an Oxford–Swindon–Bath and Bristol service was inaugurated which from the start enjoyed good passenger loadings. This service was withdrawn in May 2003, a victim of cuts made to ensure trains kept time on a busy line.

An advertisement in the *Bath & Wilts Chronicle & Herald*, 23 March 1934.

Chippenham station timetable for winter 1965/6.

(Author's Collection)

No. 1003 *County of Wilts* leaves Swindon Junction with the combined 11.40 a.m. Cheltenham–Paddington
and the 10.15 a.m. from Taunton (1.30 p.m. departure from Swindon Junction), in 1948,
seen from Swindon East signal-box.

(E.J.M. Hayward)

The prototype HST 252001, now preserved at the National Railway Museum, York,
being tested on the Up line near the site of Bathford Halt, 18 December 1974.

(C.G. Maggs)

Over the years quite a number of named trains have run over the Swindon to Bath line. The first was the 'Flying Dutchman', named after a racehorse that won both the Derby and the St Leger in 1849. It made its last broad-gauge run on 20 May 1892, and ran as an undistinguished standard-gauge train until 1911. The 'Zulu' was the unofficial name for the 3 p.m. Paddington to Plymouth service introduced in 1879 during the Zulu War. This nickname faded out in about 1914. The broad-gauge 'Cornishman', introduced in 1880, carried third-class passengers at a time when many important expresses were restricted to holders of first- and second-class tickets. It was withdrawn on 1 July 1904 when the 'Cornish Riviera Limited' was introduced, running non-stop to Plymouth via Swindon.

'The Bristolian' was inaugurated on 9 September 1935 to mark the GWR's centenary. It ran non-stop from Paddington to Temple Meads via Bath in 1 hour 45 minutes, 15 minutes faster than the previous best, and required an average speed of 67 mph. On its Up run it travelled via Badminton. Withdrawn during the Second World War, the service did not return to the 1¾ hour timing until 1954. The name was dropped in the 1960s but was reintroduced on 30 May 1999.

One of the named trains put on in 1951, Festival of Britain year, was 'The Merchant Venturer', the first named train for many years actually to stop at Bath before terminating at Bristol. It left Paddington at 11.15 a.m. and arrived at Bath Spa at 1.01 p.m. In the Up direction it was rather more sluggish, leaving Bath at 5.44 p.m. then calling at Chippenham, Swindon and slipping a coach at Reading General before arriving at Paddington at 8 p.m., its average speed a pedestrian 40 mph. The name was dropped in the 1965 timetable.

The 'Bristol Pullman', inaugurated on 3 October 1960, was hailed as a great innovation and considered unusual for several reasons. Firstly, Pullman cars were rare on

Timetable, March 1952

Metro-Vickers gas turbine No. 18100 passing through Sydney Gardens with the Down 'Merchant Venturer'.

(O.S. Nock, courtesy P.Q. Treloar)

A guard boarding the Up 'Bristol Pullman' at Bath, 22 May 1964. It temporarily consisted of locomotive-hauled stock, while the usual set was being serviced.

(C.G. Maggs)

the GWR or Western Region. Secondly, instead of being hauled by a traditional locomotive, the 'Bristol Pullman' had a power unit at each end of the train and was, in fact, a precursor of today's HSTs. Thirdly, the train's livery was blue and white, a startling departure from the standard maroon of ordinary coaching stock, or the brown and white of traditional Pullmans – in fact, it was not unlike the standard livery that BR adopted in 1965. Each power car had a North British/MAN 12-cylinder 1000-bhp diesel engine giving a maximum speed of 90 mph. Transmission was electric. Initially it did not call at Chippenham, but did on some trips in 1962. Unfortunately the ride quality of the 'Bristol Pullman' was not above criticism. It ceased running on 4 May 1973, by which time ordinary Mk IID coaches had air conditioning, rode more comfortably than the 'Bristol Pullman' cars and did not charge a Pullman supplement.

Between the world wars both the 4.15 p.m. and the 6.30 p.m. Paddington to Plymouth expresses slipped a coach at Chippenham. This was then attached to a steam railmotor calling at intermediate stations to Bath, enabling passengers to enjoy a fast run from Paddington and then continue to their local station without changing. Coaches were slipped from the main train on leaving Cocklebury cutting, just before the Calne branch Down home signal, 730 yd from the centre of Chippenham station. Occasionally a mishap occurred when the slip coach stopped short and a GWR horse was sent to tow it into the platform, and on one occasion it overshot and a shunting engine had to recover it from Thingley Junction.

About 1925 two coaches were slipped at Bath at 1 p.m. from the 11.15 a.m. Paddington to Weston-super-Mare. After arriving, two shunting horses drew them to one of the two centre roads before they were taken onwards to Bristol. Withdrawn during the Second World War, the first postwar slip arrived at Bath on 6 May 1946, the slip portion of the 9.05 a.m. Paddington to Temple Meads usually having at least three coaches.

Slip coaches from a Down express arriving at Bath in 1935, with the guard at the controls.
Note the large warning gong.

(Author's Collection)

Workmen and families for the Swindon 'Trip', 1906.
Their position beside the main line looks fraught with danger.

(Author's Collection)

When slipping a coach it was important that the vacuum in the brake system was at its highest level when the coach was released, otherwise there was insufficient vacuum in the reservoir for the brakes to be released several times. This meant that when approaching the 30 mph limit for non-stop trains through Bath, a driver had to reduce his speed well in advance and then blow the brake off well before the slip coach was detached a short distance on the Bath side of the Up advanced starter, 340 yd from the centre of Bath platform.

The 'Bath Spa Slip' began running on 1 October 1912 and brought with it an interesting innovation – a ladies' attendant to assist during the 108 minute run. This coach was reserved for Bath passengers only and seats were bookable in advance at 1s per seat. The coach was taken to Bristol by the next train and returned on the 2.10 p.m. Temple Meads to Paddington (2.35 p.m. ex-Bath) with 'Bath Spa Express' roof boards. The Reading slip coach was at the rear of this train. In order to let passengers boarding at Bath have an empty coach, all doors of the Bath coach were locked so that no one could board at Bristol.

One of the features at Swindon was the annual holiday in July for employees of the railway works. The 'Trip', as it was called, took place earlier in the year than most holidays, in order that locomotives and coaches would not be taken from paying passengers. The Trip started in 1849 and developed to such an extent that in 1908 no fewer than 24,564 workers and their families left Swindon during the early morning in twenty-two special trains to such destinations as Weymouth, Weston-super-Mare, South Wales and the West of England. To ease congestion at Swindon Junction station, Trip trains left from various locations within the works, portable steps being provided to ease mounting from ground level. In 1939 27,000 left Swindon in thirty special trains. However, with the increase in car ownership, numbers using the Trip trains dwindled and they ceased in 1960.

The Great Exhibition of 1851 provided a terrific impetus to the railway and cheap fares encouraged many to travel to London for the first time in their lives. A special left

Selection of tickets.

Bath at 6.30 a.m. on 10 July 1851, the twenty coaches carrying more than a thousand passengers. The return fare of 8s 8d enabled visitors to stay in London for four days, but because the ticket cost only about half the price of an ordinary return, luggage was restricted to a carpet bag. At least seven excursion trains were run in September, some being day returns at 5s second class, but this, plus the 1s entrance fee to the exhibition, placed them beyond the pockets of those whose weekly wage was 12s or so. Several employers paid fares for their workers to travel to London for the day. The Bath Travelling Association was formed to secure cheap excursion trains – 8s 6d for a four-day ticket. A train arranged by the association on 4 August consisted of 28 coaches and carried about 1,400 passengers. Altogether the association took about 3,000 people to the exhibition.

Several passengers illegally sold unused halves of excursion tickets. Inspector Barton overheard people on the train talking of how they had procured cheap tickets. He kept incognito, but on arrival at Swindon revealed his identity, said that he hoped they had enjoyed a good ride and offered them the opportunity of paying the full fare, or else travelling to Bristol gratis and being liable to a fine.

Problems were encountered on 3 September, the *Bath & Cheltenham Gazette* recording:

> The time announced for the departure of the train was 6.30, but as early as half-past 5, numbers of excursionists were at the station; and shortly after 6, the paying-office was completely filled with them, while hundreds were outside waiting to gain admittance. It was soon evident that the supply of carriages was insufficient, and three open goods trucks were attached to the train. The issuing of tickets long before the departure of the train was necessarily suspended, and upwards of 200 would-be excursionists were, much to their disappointment, compelled to retrace their steps homewards.

> Just previous to the departure of the train, it was discovered that several holders of tickets – notwithstanding the close 'packing' by porters, could not be accommodated, and places were given them in the express which left Bath a little before 8. Great dissatisfaction, as might be expected, was expressed by those who were disappointed of their day's trip, and many bitter – and in many cases, coarse – remarks were made by these against the Company.

Lessons were learned and for 11 September excursion tickets were issued the previous day. On that day approximately 1,700 passengers were carried in 30 coaches drawn by 3 engines.

Excursionists on 24 September experienced an hour's delay at Box as no banking engine was available, so the first half of the train had to be taken to Corsham and left there while the engines returned to Box for the remainder.

Four-day excursions to London proved popular and on Saturday 10 May 1856 a train of thirty coaches conveyed nearly 2,000 passengers from Bath to Paddington. On the Up journey, when the train reached Box Tunnel the occupants of the last coaches found they were travelling backwards – a coupling had broken. The coaches were collected and placed at the front of the train, which then continued on its way.

In the spring of 1876 the GWR received criticism from a correspondent to the *Bath Chronicle*. On 23 March it was stated that if a third-class passenger wished to go from Bath to Paddington and back in a day he was required to catch the 6.48 a.m. from Bath, stopping at all stations to Reading and reaching Paddington at 11.40 a.m. Then, unless he could return on the 1.50 p.m., he had to wait until 8.10 p.m. and arrive home at about midnight, whereas first- and second-class passengers could reach Bath in less than three hours.

PLEASE RETAIN THIS HANDBILL FOR REFERENCE

BRITISH RAILWAYS
WESTERN REGION

UNTIL FURTHER NOTICE

CHEAP DAY TICKETS

will be issued as shewn

ON WEEKDAYS and SUNDAYS

(Where train service permits)

BY ANY TRAIN

from BATH SPA

TO	RETURN FARES		TO	RETURN FARES	
	First Class	Third Class		First Class	Third Class
	s. d.	s. d.		s. d.	s. d.
BOX	1 10	1 0	KEYNSHAM & SOM.	2 5	1 5
BOX (Mill Lane)	2 1	1 3	LIMPLEY STOKE	2 4	1 5
BRADFORD-ON-AVON	3 3	2 1	PORTISHEAD	8 0	4 11
BRISTOL (Temple Meads)‡	3 11	2 5	ST. ANNE'S PARK	3 4	2 1
CHIPPENHAM	4 6	2 9	SALTFORD	1 5	0 11
CLEVEDON	9 2	5 7	SEVERN BEACH	8 2	4 11
CLIFTON DOWN	5 0	3 0	SWINDON	10 2	6 1
CORSHAM	3 1	1 11	TROWBRIDGE	4 6	2 9
DEVIZES (via Seend)	7 11	4 9	WARMINSTER	7 4	4 6
FRESHFORD	2 7	1 7	WESTBURY	5 10	3 6
FROME	7 6	4 6	WESTON-SUPER-MARE	10 7	6 4

from BATHAMPTON

TO	RETURN FARES	
	First Class	Third Class
	s. d.	s. d.
BATH SPA	0 11	0 6
BRISTOL (Temple Meads)‡	4 9	2 10
CHIPPENHAM	3 9	2 4
TROWBRIDGE	3 7	2 2

PASSENGERS RETURN BY ANY TRAIN THE SAME DAY.

‡ Passengers have the option of returning from Bristol (Stapleton Road) by direct trains.

SEE OTHER SIDE FOR PARTICULARS OF CHEAP DAY TICKETS FROM BATHFORD HALT AND OLDFIELD PARK.

PLEASE RETAIN THIS HANDBILL FOR REFERENCE

BRITISH RAILWAYS
WESTERN REGION

UNTIL FURTHER NOTICE

CHEAP DAY TICKETS

will be issued as shewn

ON WEEKDAYS and SUNDAYS

(Where train service permits)

BY ANY TRAIN

from BATHFORD HALT

TO	RETURN FARES	
	First Class	Third Class
	s. d.	s. d.
BATH SPA	0 11	0 6
BRISTOL (Temple Meads) ‡	5 0	3 0
CHIPPENHAM	3 4	2 1

from OLDFIELD PARK

TO	RETURN FARES		TO	RETURN FARES	
	First Class	Third Class		First Class	Third Class
	s. d.	s. d.		s. d.	s. d.
BOX	2 4	1 5	KEYNSHAM & SOM.	2 1	1 3
BOX (Mill Lane)	2 5	1 5	LIMPLEY STOKE	2 7	1 7
BRADFORD-ON-AVON	3 7	2 2	PORTISHEAD	7 9	4 8
BRISTOL (Temple Meads)‡	3 7	2 2	ST. ANNE'S PARK	3 1	1 11
CHIPPENHAM	4 9	2 10	SALTFORD	1 3	0 9
CLEVEDON	8 9	5 4	SEVERN BEACH	7 4	4 6
CLIFTON DOWN	4 8	2 10	SWINDON	10 7	6 4
CORSHAM	3 4	2 1	TROWBRIDGE	4 9	2 10
DEVIZES (via Seend)	8 2	4 11	WARMINSTER	7 9	4 8
FRESHFORD	3 0	1 10	WESTBURY	6 1	3 7
FROME	7 11	4 9	WESTON-SUPER-MARE	10 2	6 1

PASSENGERS RETURN BY ANY TRAIN THE SAME DAY.

‡ Passengers have the option of returning from Bristol (Stapleton Road) by direct trains.

SEE OTHER SIDE FOR PARTICULARS OF CHEAP DAY TICKETS FROM BATH SPA AND BATHAMPTON.

PASSENGERS HOLDING CHEAP DAY TICKETS ARE ALLOWED TO ALIGHT AT A STATION SHORT OF DESTINATION IN EACH DIRECTION, ON SURRENDER OF TICKET, AND TO RETURN FROM ANY INTERMEDIATE STATION.

Children under Three years of age, Free; Three and under Fourteen years of age, Half-fare.

NOTICE AS TO CONDITIONS.—These tickets are issued subject to the Conditions of issue of ordinary passenger tickets, where applicable, and also to the special Conditions as set out in the Ticket, etc., Regulations, By-laws and General Notices. Luggage allowances are as set out in these General Notices.

Tickets can be obtained in advance at booking stations and agencies.

Further information will be supplied on application to Stations, Agencies, or to Mr. L. EDWARDS, Divisional Superintendent, Temple Meads Station, Bristol, 1 (Telephone 21001, Extension 211 or 212); or Mr. C. FURBER, Commercial Superintendent, Paddington Station, London, W.2.

Paddington Station,
January, 1950.

K. W. C. GRAND,
Chief Regional Officer.

(Bristol—3,000)   Printed by J. W. Arrowsmith Ltd., Quay Street, Bristol.   (B7/41)

Handbills, January 1950.
(Author's Collection)

He revealed that 'some time ago' the GWR erected placards proclaiming in prominent type that there would be 'third class by all trains', and only on very close examination could it be read in the very small type suddenly resorted to, that almost all the trains by which ordinary people would think of travelling were excepted. The matter was resolved in June 1882 when all trains, except for two expresses each way, carried third-class passengers.

A correspondent travelled by the 12.50 a.m. Temple Meads to Paddington train on 21 March 1876 and found the carriage divided into three compartments dimly lighted by a lamp at one end, 'while the other was so dark that it was only by the help of the guard's lamp I was prevented from sitting on a passenger laid under a rug'. The centre compartment was in a filthy condition, and when he asked the guard if a better compartment was available he received a negative reply.

A correspondent to the edition of 6 April 1876 wrote:

It is not so very long since I was shown into a third class of the night train from Paddington with one lamp, more like a rush light than anything else in illuminating power, to seven compartments. The pervading gloom prevented my noticing how dirty it was. Its aspect, however, was so forbidding that I refused to travel in it and took my place in a second class compartment, in which I arrived at Bath without any further remonstrance on the part of officials.

When Guard Joan Smith worked on the 11.05 p.m. from Bath shortly after the Second World War, sometimes it took 1½ hours to reach Chippenham. The guard and assistant guard experienced difficulties getting tickets from intoxicated men at unstaffed halts and stopping them from jumping out the wrong side deliberately or accidentally. The communication cord could be pulled at Box, the 'butterflies' reset and then probably pulled again at Mill Lane. Going through Box Tunnel the cord might be pulled three times. As the fireman went back to find where the cord had been pulled, windows were open and passengers looking out. He went in fear and dread that some would vomit over him! At Corsham on one occasion the cord had been pulled in every coach. A naval officer occupied the first compartment with the Front Guard Joan Smith in case men got 'fresh' with her.

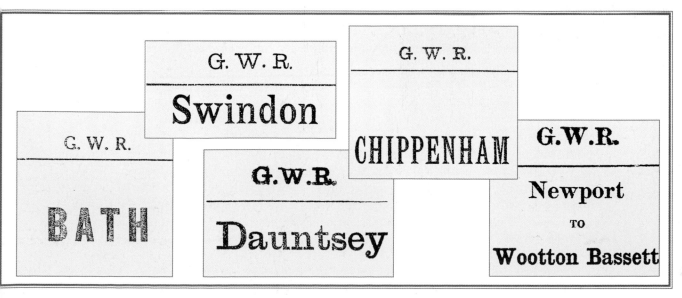

Selection of luggage labels.

Chapter Five

LOCOMOTIVES & ENGINE SHEDS

LOCOMOTIVES

The first engines mentioned as working the Swindon to Bath line were 'Sun' class 2–2–2s, being a version of the 'Fire Fly' class with 6-ft- instead of 7-ft-diameter driving wheels and therefore more suited to the line's gradients. In 1846 an enlarged 'Fire Fly', the 2–2–2 *Great Western*, appeared and ran from Paddington to Exeter in 3 hours 28 minutes compared with the 5 hours taken by a conventional 'Fire Fly'. *Great Western* had rather too much weight on its front axle, so the frames were lengthened and the wheel arrangement altered to 4–2–2. In 1847 a similar, though slightly larger, 4–2–2 engine was built. This was the 'Iron Duke' class, so-called because the first engine ran its test trip on the Duke of Wellington's birthday, 29 April. Goods trains were worked by 2–4–0s and 0–6–0s.

Apart from 'Iron Duke' renewals, from 1876 onwards, as the end of the broad-gauge era was in sight, all new engines required for the broad gauge were standard-gauge engines with broad-gauge axles. Armstrong's 0–6–0STs of the 1076 class, which appeared in 1876, were the first GWR convertibles and used as mixed-traffic engines, some of those on passenger duty being altered to 0–4–2STs to permit freer running. Owing to a shortage of broad-gauge goods engines between 1884 and 1888, twenty of Armstrong's 'Standard Goods' 0–6–0s built in 1876 were converted from standard to broad gauge and then, in 1892, back to standard gauge. When running on the broad gauge they drew old broad-gauge tenders, and as their standard-gauge-width cabs remained they presented an odd appearance. Another group of convertible engines were 2–4–0s for express duty.

Swindon decided to try a compound engine, so in 1886 No. 8, a broad-gauge 4-cylinder compound 2–4–0, appeared with a boiler pressure of 180 lb – high for the time. After teething troubles discovered when running light between Swindon and Dauntsey had seemingly been ironed out, authority had sufficient confidence to try it as pilot on the 3 p.m. Temple Meads to Paddington express. This was a heavy train and always piloted east of Bath.

On one occasion the train engine was broad-gauge 'Hawthorn' class 2–4–0 *Acheron*. At Bath, No. 8 was coupled in front, the compound driver instructing Jones, *Acheron*'s driver, to give his engine just sufficient steam to keep it going because No. 8 would do most of the work. Ten yards outside the western portal of Box Tunnel, two loud explosions and the sound of escaping steam could be heard. As E.L. Ahrons, a footplate recorder, wrote:

> It was pitch dark, and a rain of fragments of cast iron mixed with large gun-metal nuts was projected against the roof of the tunnel, from which they rebounded like shrapnel on to the footplate. The position was distinctly uncomfortable; no one could tell what had happened, but

the driver dare not shut off steam or the train would have 'stuck' on the 1 in 100 rise, for had this occurred all the efforts of Mr Jones and the *Acheron* would have been useless.

It transpired that No. 8 had smashed three of her pistons and cylinder covers. By keeping steam on, the one high-pressure cylinder remaining intact managed to keep the train moving with *Acheron*'s help. The compound was taken off at Chippenham and replaced with a goods engine. Although repaired, the same breakage reoccurred, so it was the end for this engine. However, it was never actually withdrawn from stock and in May 1894 No. 8 was officially renewed as 'simple' engine No. 8, an 'Armstrong' class 4–4–0, but it is believed that only the wheel centres came from the original compound.

The descent of Dauntsey Bank was a good speeding ground. Brunel and Charles Sacré tested Gooch's 'Iron Duke' class engines when new. Driven flat-out, *Iron Duke*, *Courier* and *Great Britain* all reached 78 mph, while down the bank ordinary expresses with steam off reached 60 mph. It was here that on 14 July 1903 No. 3433 *City of Bath*, hauling 130 tons on the first non-stop run from Paddington to Plymouth, reached 87 mph, while about thirty years later No. 6018 *King Henry VI*, with seven coaches, 236 tons tare, achieved 102½ mph at milepost 87, ¾ mile before Dauntsey.

Practically all classes of standard-gauge GWR engines worked over the line at one time or another. Towards the end of the nineteenth century express passenger trains were hauled by engines of the 2–4–0, 2–2–2 and 4–2–2 wheel arrangement, goods trains by 0–6–0s and stopping passengers by 2–4–0Ts or 0–4–2Ts. 'Sir Daniel' class 2–2–2s worked the 9.35 a.m. express Bristol to Paddington and two trains Bristol to Swindon, but then as heavier loads demanded four-coupled machines, and the 'Sir Daniels' were virtually the same as the Armstrong 'Standard Goods' apart from the wheel arrangement,

'Queen' class 2–2–2 No. 1131 standing on one of the middle roads at Bath, *c.* 1900.
Built in 1875, she was withdrawn in 1905.

(*W. Vaughan Jenkins*)

'Armstrong' class 4–4–0 No. 16 *Brunel* at Bath with a Down stopping train, its driver taking the opportunity
to oil the inside cylinders. Originally a broad-gauge 2–4–0, *Brunel* was built in 1888
for working the heavy 3 p.m. Temple Meads–Swindon.

(Author's Collection)

they were converted to 0–6–0s. Their curved frames were retained, giving them a
distinctly odd appearance, as they had originally been above the 7-ft-diameter driving
wheels. In the 1890s No. 9, a 2–2–2, worked slow trains from Bristol to Swindon;
considered a strong engine, it was easily recognisable because its valve gear was,
unusually, placed outside the frames.

In 1894 Dean's 'Armstrong' class 4–4–0s appeared and worked the heavier expresses,
rather than the 'Achilles' class 4–2–2s which encountered problems with the increasingly
heavy trains and were only just capable of hauling eight coaches up through Box Tunnel.

From 1901 the speedy 'City' class 4–4–0s monopolised the Paddington to Penzance
expresses. The 4–4–0 'County' class appeared on West of England expresses in 1904.
Otherwise similar in dimensions to the 'City' class, their cylinder stroke was 4 in longer
and the cylinders placed outside, rather than inside. Although satisfactory from the power
point of view, their large outside cylinders and short wheelbase caused them to roll badly
and earned them the nickname 'Churchward's Rough Riders'. They were soon
superseded on main-line expresses by 4–6–0s and all were withdrawn by 1932.

Two-cylinder 4–6–0 No. 10 (later No. 2900) *William Dean* appeared in 1902 and it,
along with the remainder of the 'Saint' class, took over West of England expresses from
the 4–4–0s. No. 171 (later No. 2971) *Albion* appeared in 1903 as an Atlantic, in order to
give a better comparison with No. 102 *La France*. This 4-cylinder de Glehn compound
4–4–2, purchased in 1903, was followed by the larger No. 103 *President* and No. 104
Alliance in 1905, and initially worked through Swindon on West of England's expresses.

Churchward built a 'simple' engine with the de Glehn cylinder arrangement and
produced a masterpiece that was the basis of all subsequent large GWR passenger

De Glehn compound 4–4–2 No. 104 *Alliance* heading an Up express at Bath, *c.* 1910. A train stands
in the adjacent bay platform. No. 104 was built at Belfort, France, in 1905 and withdrawn in 1928.

(Author's Collection)

De Glehn compound 4–4–2 No. 103, named *President* in 1907, with an Up stopping train at Bath, *c.* 1906.
No. 103 was built at Belfort in 1905 and withdrawn in 1927.

(Author's Collection)

In order to make a better comparison between standard GWR locomotives and 'The Frenchmen', No. 179 *Magnet*, named after a stagecoach, and later renumbered No. 2979 *Quintin Durward*, was built as a 4–4–2. Here she stands on the Up road at Bath, *c.* 1905.

(Author's Collection)

engines. No. 40 (later No. 4000) *North Star* appeared as a 4–4–2 in 1906 for comparison with the French Atlantics (built in France), but was converted to a 4–6–0 in 1909. The 'Star' class immediately became the principal express engines. A super 'Star', Pacific No.111 *The Great Bear*, appeared in 1908 but was simply for prestige, as its wheels and mechanical parts were standard with the 'Stars', the difference being a larger boiler and firebox. Its weight restricted it to the Paddington to Bristol road and it tended to work an express passenger in one direction and return with a vacuum-fitted goods train. In 1924 it was rebuilt as a 'Castle'. The 'Castle' class 4–6–0s had appeared in 1923 and were followed by 'Kings' four years later. Both were used on Paddington to Bristol expresses, 'Kings' hauling the heavier trains but 'Castles' being faster and favourites for 'The Bristolian'.

With the craze for streamlining in the 1930s No. 5005 *Manorbier Castle* had appurtenances added in March 1935, as did No. 6014 *King Henry VII*. The 4–6–0 'County' class appeared from 1945 and, new from the works, often appeared on a Swindon to Bristol running-in turn. For the locomotive enthusiast these were the most interesting trains, the postwar timings being:

7.35 a.m.	Swindon–Bristol
10.05 a.m.	Bristol–Swindon
5 p.m.	Swindon–Bristol
8.25 p.m.	Bristol–Swindon

'Castle' class 4–6–0 No. 7037 *Swindon* on the middle road, Bath, with an Up running-in turn, 26 May 1953.

(The Revd Alan Newman)

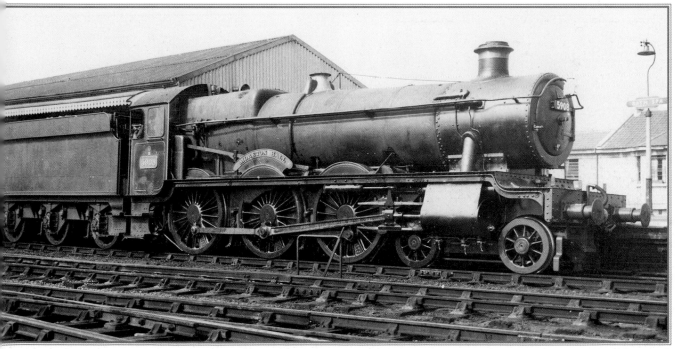

No. 5908 *Moreton Hall* with an Up running-in turn, 25 March 1953.
The tender still carries the 1934 'shirt button' monogram.

(The Revd Alan Newman)

Stanier class 5MT 2–6–0
No. 42978 at Chippenham,
working the 5.25 a.m.
Westbury–Swindon
stopping train, a running-in
turn, 1964. During this
period engines of this
class were repaired at
Swindon Works.

(Christopher Kent)

4–4–0 No. 3440 *City of Truro*, now preserved by the National Railway Museum, arrives at Bath
on 19 May 1957 with a Down excursion. Notice the concrete signalpost on the right.
On the left is a 'devil' to prevent the water column freezing.

(R.E. Toop)

A variety of new tender engines, or those out-shopped after overhaul, appeared with their smell of new paint. An engine normally worked for three days before despatch to its home shed. On 25 March 1957 No. 3440 *City of Truro* appeared for its three-day stint. Ex-works tank engines sometimes appeared on the 4.07 p.m. stopping train from Swindon, returning the following day on the 1.10 p.m. Temple Meads to Swindon.

Until about 1900 goods trains were mainly handled by 0–6–0s of the tender or tank variety, but that year the 'Aberdare' class 2–6–0s appeared and initially were employed on heavy coal trains between Aberdare and Swindon. However, they were soon eclipsed by the 2–8–0s which appeared in 1903. The first engines of that wheel arrangement in Britain, they were so successful that they continued to be built for the next thirty-nine years. Freight trains were also headed by the mixed-traffic 43XX 2–6–0s and later by 'Hall' and 'Grange' class 4–6–0s.

In June 1946 No. 5953 *Garth Hall* was converted to oil burning, renumbered 3950 and appeared on the running-in trains. Ten others of the 'Hall' class were converted, as were five 'Castles' and twenty of the 28XX class. The intention had been to convert more locomotives, but the scheme had to be abandoned owing to the postwar shortage of foreign currency. By 1950 all had been converted back to burning coal.

In 1907 the 5.30 a.m. newspaper and mail train from Paddington was worked to Temple Meads by a 'County' tank, the 4–4–2T arriving at 8.28 a.m. It returned on the 9.35 a.m. 'Weston-super-Mare Express' from Bristol, which arrived at Paddington at 12.20 p.m. The water pick-up apparatus on this class was designed to raise water whether running chimney- or bunker-first.

Ninety-nine railmotors appeared between October 1903 and February 1908, though the class did not prove an unqualified success. Firing could only be done with the regulator closed, so this meant that if there was no down gradient, a fireman could only fire when steam was shut off at the approach to a station, or when actually stopped. Another weakness was the loss of steam not only through strained steam delivery pipes adjacent to the steam chest, but also through leaking tubes. Although the cars had a good turn of speed when running alone, jerking was felt when hauling a trailer. Railmotors from various local sheds worked between Bath and Swindon, one even coming from as far afield as Yatton. Fireman Arthur Cannings of Bath lost a stone in weight firing railmotors in summer because they were so hot.

Several 'foreign' engines have appeared on the line. In about 1903 Great Central Railway 4–4–2 No. 102 worked over the line with a train from Manchester to Plymouth, a trip of 374 miles each way. In 1904 and 1905 GCR No. 267 repeated this feat. In the autumn of 1926 the LMS borrowed No. 5000 *Launceston Castle* for trials between Euston and Carlisle. In exchange 4–4–0 class 4P Compound No. 1047 was stationed at Bristol, Bath Road shed for three weeks. Just for the first week she worked the 9.15 a.m. Temple Meads to Paddington and the 1.15 p.m. Paddington to Temple Meads with a two-hour timing. During the Second World War USA-built S160 class and War Department 2–8–0s appeared.

The first BR Standard class to appear on the line was the class 7 'Britannia', those initially allocated to the Western Region having names of broad-gauge locomotives. In the mid-1950s 'Castles' and 'Kings' were fitted with four-row superheaters and double chimneys which made the excellent engines even more economical.

In June 1947 the GWR's general manager, Sir James Milne, and his chief mechanical engineer, Frederick W. Hawksworth, attended the International Railway Congress at Lucerne and visited Brown Boveri's works at Baden. Impressed by the gas-turbine

Brown-Boveri gas turbine locomotive No. 18000 entering Bath with an Up express, 11 May 1951.

(The Revd Alan Newman)

No. 31115 heading a Down parcels train at Bath, 26 February 1976.

(C.G. Maggs)

'Adelante' No. 180105 works an
Up empty coaching stock train at
Bathampton, 10 April 2002.

(C.G. Maggs)

locomotive, they ordered a 2500-hp A1A–A1A machine with a maximum tractive effort of 31,500 lb. It was not delivered until 3 February 1950, when it received the number 18000. After teething troubles it regularly worked from Paddington to Bristol. Efficient when working at full power up gradients, it displayed greatly reduced efficiency on less than full power – which was how it worked for most of the time.

A similar machine was ordered from Metropolitan-Vickers Electrical Company Ltd. No. 18100 was delivered to Swindon on 16 December 1951 and taken into stock in April 1952, its maximum tractive effort of 60,000 lb making it the most powerful engine in the country.

Unfortunately both engines were mechanically unreliable and used almost as much fuel idling, or running under reduced power, as under full load. No. 18100 was withdrawn in January 1958 and 18000 in December 1960.

On 18 August 1958 driver training began with BR Gloucester Carriage & Wagon Company railcars. From 6 April 1959 stopping trains between Swindon and Weston-super-Mare were DMU-operated.

Diesel-hydraulic D600 *Active* 'Warship' class made a demonstration run from Paddington to Bristol on 17 February 1958, reaching 94 mph down Dauntsey Bank and having no difficulty in keeping the timings. The class appeared on 'The Bristolian' in August 1959. In 1961 the 'Western' diesel-hydraulics (class 52) appeared from Swindon Works. Between 1968 and 1969 a Brush-built diesel-electric comparable with the 'Westerns' arrived on the scene. Named *Falcon*, it worked Paddington to Bristol expresses. Class 50s made redundant by the LMR's West Coast electrification superseded 'Westerns' on Bristol to Paddington trains on 6 May 1974. Then, following trial runs between Temple Meads and Paddington from 16 to 19 December 1974, HST (High Speed Train) No. 252001 appeared on some trains in 1975, a regular service starting in the spring of 1977. The HSTs proved a great success and within a few months patronage rose by nearly 18 per cent. Two 'Adelante' trains were placed on the Paddington to Temple Meads service on 2 June 2002.

The engine house, Swindon, 1846.

(Engraving by J.C. Bourne)

Swindon shed, 2 June 1935: No. 5010 *Restormel Castle*; an unidentified 2–6–0;
streamlined No. 5005 *Manorbier Castle*; a 'Saint'; an ROD class 2–8–0; and a 2–6–0.

(P.Q. Treloar Collection)

LOCOMOTIVE SHEDS

Swindon

The original broad-gauge locomotive shed at Swindon, near the junction of the Bath and Gloucester lines, was officially opened on 1 January 1843. Constructed of timber, apart from stone corners, it held a total of forty-eight tender engines. Set at right angles was another shed holding thirty-six locomotives. The shed closed in May 1892 with the abolition of the broad gauge and became part of the works. In 1871 a nine-road standard-gauge shed was built on the Up side of the Gloucester line. In 1908 a turntable shed was added to the east. Swindon shed closed in October 1964.

Hay Lane

When the line opened to Hay Lane, a temporary locomotive depot opened in December 1840 and closed in about 1842. It only offered sidings and facilities for water and cleaning smokeboxes and ashpans.

Chippenham

The shed partly opened in April 1857 and was fully open that August. The stone-walled, slated roof building had three roads. The depot closed on 2 March 1964.

Swindon shed, May 1964: ex-Somerset & Dorset Joint Railway class 7F 2–8–0 No. 53807,
sent for minor repairs before working a Bournemouth–Bath special on 7 June 1964,
and Ivatt class 4MT 2–6–0 No. 43056. This latter class was regularly repaired at Swindon.

(Colin Roberts)

'Bulldog' class 4–4–0 No. 3370 *Tremayne* at Chippenham shed, *c*. 1908.
The surprisingly clean coal stage and locomotive coal wagon are on the right.

(Edward Spearing Collection)

Chippenham locomotive depot, *c*. 1908: beside the ash piles is a 2–4–0T or 0–4–2T, while on the right is a
'Standard Goods' 0–6–0, probably No. 601. Note the rings on the tender for supporting the emergency cord.
Locomotive coal wagon No. 9087 is by the coal stage.

(Edward Spearing Collection)

Hymek diesel electric D7074 passes Chippenham engine shed on 1 February 1964 with the 1.45 a.m. Tavistock Junction–Swindon goods, including 45XX class 2–6–2T No. 4564 with some of its motion dismantled. It had lain idle at St Blazey shed since working a railtour in April 1962, then worked at Gloucester during the spring and summer of 1964, and was officially withdrawn in September 1964.

(Christopher Kent)

Box

Open-air facilities for a banking engine were provided until a single-road, timber-built shed set on low stone walls was constructed by Thomas Lewis for £328 10s. Completed early in 1842, it enjoyed restricted use until a water supply was provided in 1845.

The Box engine was changed weekly, a fresh one coming from Swindon via Chippenham shed. Only some freight trains were banked through the tunnel, such as the 'Southall' and *The Great Bear* on Fry's cocoa train, which if it had an overload would be assisted through to Wootton Bassett. As tank engines were prohibited from piloting, the banker would be put inside *The Great Bear*. With more powerful engines provided on trains there was less need for a banking engine and the shed closed on 24 February 1919. From that date, if required, a banking engine was sent from Chippenham.

Bath

The original single-road locomotive shed at Bath, east of the Up passenger platform, opened in August 1840. Its design is unknown, but was probably similar to that at Box. Access was across a 35 ft turntable. The shed closed in November 1880 and was replaced by one at the Westmoreland goods yard on the Bristol side of the station.

'Dean Goods' class 0–6–0 No. 2314 outside Box engine shed, *c.* 1910.
Notice it stands on 15-ft-length flat-bottomed rail.

(H. Foster/M.J. Tozer Collection)

LOCOMOTIVE ALLOCATIONS
Chippenham, 25 April 1857

Gooch 'Standard Goods' 0–6–0
Pallas
Thames

19 July 1862

'Victoria' class 2–4–0
Abdul Medjid
Gooch 'Standard Goods' 0–6–0
Nero

1 January 1921

850 class 0–6–0T
858
1076 class 0–6–0T
1257
1289
2021 class 0–6–0T
2060
'Dean Goods' 0–6–0
2571
Steam railmotor
63

31 December 1947

Collett 0–4–2T
1433
1453
8750 class 0–6–0PT
3684
3748
4651
8779
9720
9721

Box, March 1842

'Leo' class 2–4–0
Aries

1854–61

'Banking' class 0–6–0ST
Avalanche
Bithon
Jago
Pluto

19 July 1862

'Banking' class 0–6–0ST

Bithon

Juno

Bath, 1840s

'Sun' class 2–2–2

Sun

'Fire Fly' class 2–2–2

Fire King

1850s

'Bogie' class 4–4–0ST

Homer

Chapter Six

PERMANENT WAY & SIGNALLING

PERMANENT WAY

The original double-track permanent way was 62 lb per yd bridge rail laid on longitudinal sleepers 14 in × 7 in set to a gauge of 7 ft ¼ in. Because it was continuously supported, bridge rail, so-named because of its inverted 'U' cross-section, had the advantage of being lighter and therefore cheaper than the usual bullhead rail used by other railways. Sir John Wolfe-Barry, consulting engineer and founder of the Engineering Standards Committee, writing in 1876 stated that Brunel's 62 lb per yd rail equalled 75–80 lb per yd bullhead rail laid on transome sleepers.

In order to satisfy critics who envisaged trains running away on the Down line through Box Tunnel, instead of bridge rails in this situation, Brunel used two flat, iron plates 7 in wide and ¾ in thick, laid on a thick layer of compressible felt and slightly inclined inwards. It proved an unnecessary precaution and the Down line was entirely relaid with conventional track in June 1851, for eight days all trains being worked over the Up line.

Swindon to Thingley Junction and Bath to Bristol were converted to mixed gauge in June 1874, the intervening length from Thingley Junction to Bathampton becoming mixed gauge on 1 March 1875. The broad-gauge rails continued to be used by through trains to Devon and Cornwall until the end of the broad-gauge era. The last public broad-gauge train was the Up mail which left Temple Meads at 12.45 a.m. on 21 May 1892 hauled by 4–2–2 *Bulkeley*. Thirteen special trains conveying broad-gauge rolling stock from Cornwall and Devon passed later that night en route for scrapping or conversion at Swindon, while some broad-gauge coaches were placed in sidings at Exeter to be hauled to Swindon later, as the broad-gauge rail of the mixed gauge east of Exeter was not immediately lifted, though it had certainly been removed by the end of 1892.

Permanent-way gangs usually consisted of five men: a ganger, sub-ganger and three lengthmen.

Gangs, 1950

Name of Gang	Length
Swindon	Swindon–Hay Lane
Hay Lane	Hay Lane–Wootton Bassett
Wootton Bassett	Wootton Bassett–Tockenham Bridge
Dauntsey	Tockenham Bridge–Friday Street Bridge (between Dauntsey and Christian Malford)
Christian Malford	Friday Street Bridge–Avon Bridge
Langley	Avon Bridge–Langley
Chippenham	Langley–Thingley Junction

As soon as a Train has entered the Tunnel, the Policeman must turn on his Cross Bar or Red Light, and then the information will be first communicated by him to the man at the further Tunnel mouth, in the following manner, he is to ring the bell the number of times specified to call attention, wait till the same number of Bells is returned, then pull out the stop, turn the right-hand index to T., push in the stop, and work the hand round till the short end points to the number on the dial referring to the desired message, the party receiving the message then works the hand round to the letters Q.S. to signify the signal has been understood, after which the party who sent the signal works round to the M., pulls out the stop, turns the right-hand index to B., pushes in the stop, and the instrument is then ready for another communication.

The Cross Bar or Red Light, remains on till information is received that the Train has passed out of the Tunnel. The Policeman will then turn on his caution signal, and admit the next train, without waiting the customary ten minutes as at present with the down trains to ensure the Tunnel being clear. At the proper time (see Police Instructions) the green light will be turned off, and the white light put on.

In the event of any doubt arising in the mind of the person receiving a message, the letters Q.R. being given will signify 'it is to be repeated'.

List of Signals	No. on Dial
Up Train has entered Tunnel	12
Up Train is through Tunnel	5
Down Train has entered Tunnel	9
Down Train is out of Tunnel	3
Bank Engine has entered Tunnel	17
Bank Engine is through Tunnel	15
Wagons* are coming through Tunnel on Up Line	19
Wagons are coming through Tunnel on Down Line	18
Wagons are through Tunnel on Up Line	10
Wagons are through Tunnel on Down Line	7

* Presumably this meant a goods train with a locomotive attached.

By August 1849 the telegraph was reported as 'out of order'.

Cooke's absolute block system was introduced between Corsham and Box in 1850. When a train was ready to leave a station the next station received a 'Call Attention' sign by moving the telegraph needle once to the left, once to the right and simultaneously ringing an electric bell. It was acknowledged by moving the needle a certain number of times to the right, indicating 'Line Clear', or to the left for 'Not Clear'. In June 1852 the Electric Telegraph Company's representative found the system useless owing to defective insulation caused by the wires being 'in a water drain for half-a-mile and hung on a damp wall the rest of the way'. He advised two new wires were essential, and these were installed. In later years the block bells and telegraph wires did not pass through Box Tunnel, but were carried over the top of the hill. In 1867 the GWR telegraph superintendent C.E. Spagnoletti's disc block instruments replaced the single-needle telegraph through the tunnel.

In 1852 the time-interval system on the rest of the line was modified to: after a passenger train, 5 minutes at Danger and 5 at Caution; and after a goods, 8 minutes at Danger and 7 at Caution. The time-interval system lasted until 1877, when it was replaced by the block. In about 1874 signal-boxes were brought into use between

69

BOX TUNNEL.

SPECIAL INSTRUCTIONS FOR WORKING TRAINS THROUGH

BOX TUNNEL

Incline between Box and Corsham through the Tunnel.

1. The Up and Down Lines between Box Station and the Corsham End of the Tunnel are on a gradient of 1 in 100 rising toward Corsham, and this Incline must be worked in accordance with the Standard instructions for working Inclines and with the Book of Rules and Regulations where not specially provided for by the following additional Regulations :— *Gradient.*

The name of the Signal Box situated on the Down Line side near the Tunnel mouth at the Corsham Station end is "Tunnel East Box." *Name of Box at the Corsham end of Tunnel.*

Enginemen of Up Trains must not attempt to get through the Tunnel if they have any doubt of being able to do so, but must stop at Box Station, divide the Train (Passenger or Goods) or wait for the Box or other assistant Engine, as instructed by the Officer in charge of the Station. Should a Train come to a stand in the Tunnel the Guards must see that before it is separated the rear of the Train is properly secured. *Trains to stop at Box if Drivers have doubt about being able to get through Tunnel.*

Lights on Trains.

2. **Carriage Roof-Lamps to be Lighted.**—The Roof-Lamps of all Passenger Trains working through the Tunnel must be lighted before the Trains leave the last Lamping Station previous to entering the Tunnel, and extinguished at the first convenient Station after the Trains are through the Tunnel unless the lights will be required before the Trains reach their destination. Gas Roof-Lamps must be lighted—on the bye-pass only by day—before leaving the Starting Station *Where Roof-Lamps are to be lighted.*

3. **Train and Guards' Lamps.**—All Trains must exhibit the usual lighted Head, Side, and Tail Lamps through the Tunnel by day as well as by night; and all Engines running light must also exhibit the usual lighted Head and Tail Lamps. *All Trains to have lighted Side and Tail and Head Lamps through Tunnel.*

Guards must light their Hand lamps before reaching the Tunnel, and keep them lighted while running through. *Guards to light Hand Lamps for Tunnel.*

Loading of Up Trains through Tunnel.

4. **Maximum Loads.**—The maximum loads of Up Trains with one Engine through the Tunnel are as under :—

PASSENGER TRAINS—

Engines of 3001 class	72 wheels
Side Tank Passenger Engines	72 „
Coupled Tender Passenger Engines, 806 class	80 „
Other large Passenger Engines	96 „

GOODS TRAINS—

Trains assisted up Box Incline :—

	Coal.	Goods.	Empties.
2—8—0 Engine	63	90	100
2—6—0 Engines	50	70	80
Ordinary Tender and Tank Engines	40	50	60

Trains stopping at Box :—

	Coal.	Goods.	Empties.
2—8—0 Engine	39	55	78
2—6—0 Engine	33	49	60
Ordinary Tender Engine	20	33	45
Ordinary Tank Engine	22	36	45

Trains not stopping at Box :—

	Coal.	Goods.	Empties.
Ordinary Tender Engine	22	35	46
Ordinary Tank Engine	24	37	48

Loading of Down Trains.

	Coal.	Goods.	Empties.
2—8—0 Engine	72	85	100
2—6—2 Engine T	60	80	100
2—6—0 Engine	60	80	100
Ordinary Tender or Tank Engine	50	60	60

Special instructions for working trains through Box Tunnel.
(*Appendix to the No. 4 Section Service Time Table*, March 1910)

Paddington and Bristol, working a mixture of disc-and-crossbar and semaphore signals. The early semaphore signals at Swindon were made by Saxby & Farmer and their operating wires were carried overhead, instead of at ground level, giving a more direct route.

One of the first locking frames made at the GWR signal works at Reading was installed at Thingley Junction in the 1860s. When William Yolland inspected the mixed-gauge Bristol to Swindon line in November 1875 he wrote: 'In many signal boxes diagrams still require erecting and numbers painted on the levers to show order in which they must be worked. Generally the interlocking is well done.'

Automatic Train Control installed in the early 1930s was the next great signalling improvement, whereby a driver received an audible signal as to whether a distant signal was at Caution or Clear.

Multiple Aspect Signalling introduced in the 1960s caused signal-boxes to be closed. In preparation for HST services signalling allowed reversible working, which reduced delays when single-line working was necessary at weekends to bypass sections of track undergoing maintenance.

Owing to the length of Box Tunnel and because the rising gradient sometimes brought Up trains to a halt, towards the end of the nineteenth century a warning wire was fixed to the tunnel wall on the Up side about 5 ft from the ground. When broken, this wire rang a telltale bell in Corsham and Box signal-boxes, and on hearing it the signalman stopped all trains entering the tunnel. In the event of a train under any circumstances stopping in the tunnel, the guard was required to cut the wire. It then had to be coiled into a large loop to prevent the metal inside the insulated covering from touching the ground or wet wall, which would cause the bell to cease ringing. If tunnel

Bathampton, view Up, 16 July 1969. This box opened on 21 September 1956 and closed on 17 August 1970.
(Derrick Payne)

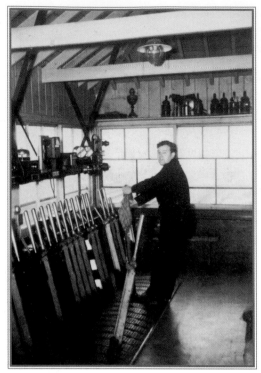

Signalman Norman Whalley in Corsham signal-box, 1960.

(Norman Whalley Collection)

Norman Whalley maintains the lamp on Corsham Down inner Home signal in 1963. The view from the public footbridge. The Station Hotel is in the background.

(Norman Whalley Collection)

workmen found anything to render the tunnel unsafe, they too were required to break the wire. Until the broken wire was repaired by the lineman, trains about to enter the tunnel had to be advised that the wire was inoperative. The warning wire was removed when MAS was installed. The signalman at Box station was required to record the time taken for a train from Corsham, and if this was over 8 minutes for a passenger, 15 minutes for a perishable, or 20 minutes for a goods, an Up train must not be allowed to pass his box.

The engineering department had three telephones set at intervals in the tunnel. The lengthman used each of these phones daily to test that they were working, and the Corsham signalman entered this fact in the train register. Today eight phones are available and set in lighted manholes. The platelayer/patrolman passing through the tunnel presses a plunger, lifts each handset and reports to Bristol Panel Box to check that each phone is working. He carries a spare lamp bulb.

As Chippenham East and Chippenham West boxes were only 572 yd apart, that is, only about half the braking distance required by a train, Chippenham West could not give 'Line Clear' for a Down train until 'Line Clear' was obtained from Thingley Junction.

The signalman at Box needed to be particularly alert when a Down train was approaching and the previous train had not cleared the section to Bathampton. As Middle Hill Tunnel was so close, he only had a few seconds to determine if the approaching train was going to stop at the home signal, or was going to overrun – in which case he had to pull the detonator lever. Although the Down home was about half the standard height, in order for it to be seen through the tunnel, it was still quite difficult for a driver to see.

SELF-ACTING CATCHPOINTS

Location (all on the Up Line)	Gradient
3,600 ft in rear of Home signal for Wootton Bassett West box	1 in 660
1,320 ft in advance of Dauntsey Up Advanced Starter near milepost 87¼	1 in 100
1,500 ft in rear of Home signal for Pictor's Siding between Middle Hill and Box tunnels*	1 in 120

* This was put in after 1911, as in the *Appendix to No. 4 Section of the Service Time Table*, published that year, Middle Hill Tunnel siding points were required to be kept open when an Up goods train was passing through Box Tunnel.

Special instructions were issued for working trains through Box Tunnel. *The Appendix to Section 4 of the Working Time Table* May 1931 stated:

Enginemen of Up Trains must not attempt to get through the Tunnel if they have any doubt of being able to do so, but must stop at Box Station, divide the Train (Passenger or Goods) or wait for the Box or other assistant engine, as instructed by the person in charge of the Station. Should a Train come to a stand in the Tunnel the Guards must see that before it is separated the rear of the Train is properly secured. A Corridor Train must never be divided in the Tunnel, but the Engine of a Corridor Train may be detached and run forward for assistance. If there is only one guard, the fireman must remain at the front of the train and the engine driver run on his own.

Chapter Seven

ACCIDENTS

_____

A great variety of accidents occurred on the Swindon to Bath line, mainly during its first seventy years, and it is worth detailing them because lessons were learned and helped make rail travel much safer. They also give valuable insight into the railway practice of the period.

One of the first accidents on the line occurred when a small slip to an embankment on Wootton Bassett incline at milepost 87 displaced the rails during the night of 8 September 1841. The Up Mail consisted of three coaches drawn by 'Star' class 2–2–2 *Rising Star* and 'Fire Fly' class 2–2–2 *Tiger*. *Rising Star* passed the slip but *Tiger* derailed, fortunately turning towards the Down line instead of down the embankment. Owing to the inherent stability of the broad gauge all the carriages remained on their wheels, but the first two were badly damaged; one passenger had his leg broken and others on the train were bruised or cut by broken window glass. As soon as the news reached London Seymour Clarke, secretary of the GWR, together with some directors, proceeded to the spot 'and saw that proper attention was given to the sufferers'. After a delay of about three hours the line was cleared and the guards and locomotive crews had sufficiently recovered to continue. The *Bath & Cheltenham Gazette* of 14 September commented: 'Too much praise cannot be given to Mr Hutchinson, the superintendent of Wootton Bassett station, for his promptitude, kindness, and attention to all passengers upon the occasion.'

On 14 August 1843 a mishap occurred to the banking engine, for an entry in the Directors' Minute Book recorded:

> Crooke the Engine Driver and Coker the Fireman of the Bank Engine at Box were called in and examined upon a charge of having been asleep while on duty – and then passing out of the siding at full speed after the Goods train had gone on, and overtaking it where it had stopped at the bottom of the incline, running into it with considerable violence and damaging several trucks. Offence was clearly proved and fact of being asleep admitted by both – dismissed.

On 14 February 1848, as an Up express ran over the high embankment west of Chippenham, a tyre came off and penetrated the floor of a coach which was fortunately unoccupied. At that period a loose tyre was not an isolated occurrence.

On 20 September 1850 a cheap excursion train from Bath was returning from Paddington. It stopped at Swindon for a locomotive change, as was the custom, and *Ajax*, a 'Premier' class 0–6–0 goods engine, was placed at the head of the train. At about 11.30 a.m., just beyond Wootton Bassett station and running at 25–30 mph, the passengers felt a tremendous concussion. The train had collided with a horsebox which a south-easterly wind had blown down a gradient of 1 in 660. 'The engine and the first four carriages were precipitated down the embankment into a field of mangold-worzel. The first carriage was turned on its side. Its roof had to be broken with a sledge hammer

An advertisement for a cheap excursion train from Bath to London, 18 September 1850. *(Bath & Cheltenham Gazette)*

GREAT WESTERN RAILWAY.
CHEAP EXCURSION TRAIN to LONDON
and BACK, on FRIDAY NEXT, the 20th SEPT.
An Excursion Train will leave BATH at 6.30, AM.,
and return the same Evening at 7.45 o'Clock.
FARES:—*From BATH to LONDON and BACK, 9s.
and 5s., in Closed Carriages,*
Passengers having Luggage will only be conveyed at
the Ordinary Fare.
Tickets may be now purchased at the Bath Station of
the Great Western Railway Company.

to get its occupants out. The screams of the female passengers was [*sic*] heart-rending' (*Bath Chronicle*, 26 September). Fortunately the coupling chain behind the fourth coach snapped, so the remainder of the train did not fall on the wrecked coaches and cause loss of life.

The Down Mail reached Wootton Bassett at 12.15 a.m. and was delayed for three hours. Some of the undamaged coaches of the excursion train were coupled to the Mail and it proceeded westwards on the Up line. Messrs Brotherhood of Chippenham cleared the wreckage and reinstated the track.

William White, the policeman (a forerunner of a signalman) on duty at Wootton Bassett, was immediately placed in custody. The case was heard before the county magistrate at the Goddard Arms, Swindon. White had been verbally advised by Skull, the day policeman, that the horsebox was secure, but White had not personally checked that it was correctly scotched with triangular pieces of wood on both sides of the wheels. A public footpath crossed the line by the horsebox and a person could have removed the scotches. Nevertheless, White was found guilty of neglect and imprisoned for two months.

The GWR learned from this accident, and also from a similar event at Shrivenham on 10 May 1848. It installed scotch blocks with padlocks at all locations where a main line needed protection, and in the 1870s further improved safety by providing trap points.

The Dauntsey Incline of 1 in 100, combined with the time-interval system of working, caused an accident on 3 January 1852. An Up goods arrived at Chippenham 20 minutes late, so the stationmaster shunted it into a siding to allow the Up Mail a clear run. As the Mail had not arrived at 1.15 a.m. (it had been delayed on the South Devon Railway), and was therefore at least 35 minutes overdue, the stationmaster despatched the goods. As there was no telegraph he had no notion of the Mail's whereabouts. Some 15 minutes after the goods left the Mail arrived, and after 5 minutes at Chippenham station continued on its way. As 20 minutes was considered sufficient time for the goods to get 'far in advance' the stationmaster did not caution the driver.

Fog had caused the rails on Dauntsey Bank to become slippery and the heavy goods train lost adhesion and almost came to a stop. That same fog obscured the rear lamps on the guard's van, and the Mail crashed into it at 50 mph. The Mail fireman and the goods guard leaped from the train before the collision, but Driver Ellis on the Mail remained at his post and received fatal injuries.

Owing to the stability of the broad gauge, only a few passengers were injured. Some even remained asleep through the event and only woke after the train had returned to Chippenham. Quite unaware that they had been to Dauntsey and back, they complained at the lengthy time the train had spent at Chippenham!

On 4 December 1862, as the goods train due at Bath at 12.30 a.m. was descending Dauntsey Bank, the axle of a truck laden with iron snapped. The wagon was derailed, together with thirteen others. The Up line was cleared on 5 December and the Down line on the 6th.

A rather lax method of carrying out permanent-way repairs caused an accident on 15 March 1865 between Bathampton and Hampton Row. Platelayers waited for the Down express due at Bath at 12.05 p.m. to pass and then removed three lengths of rail and sleepers. At 2 p.m. they left for their dinner.

The Down goods due at Bath at 11.10 a.m. had been delayed for three hours, having been shunted many times to let other trains pass. Before it reached the gap in the rails its driver spotted the danger, tried to stop, but did not succeed before the engine, tender and four wagons were derailed. The platelayers arrived on the scene and a messenger was sent to Bath for further assistance. Inspector Burton and a large gang came from Bristol. The Up line was undamaged and traffic worked both ways over this.

Henry Bailey, foreman platelayer, was taken into custody and on 16 March appeared before Bath magistrates charged with the removal of rails contrary to orders. The rule book stated that before removing a rail a man must be sent a mile along the line with a red flag, whereas Bailey only sent one after a rail had been removed and that man had only covered 300 yd before the goods train appeared. Bailey expressed deep regret for his negligence and was fined £10 plus costs, or two months' imprisonment; he paid the fine. The mayor, chairman of the magistrates, said that the GWR should not employ men 'advanced in years, but those who had their wits about them'.

On 6 November 1871 the 6.35 a.m. goods ex-Weymouth left Chippenham 15 minutes late, was held at Wootton Bassett to allow the market goods train to pass, and left Wootton Bassett with thirty-three wagons and a brake van about an hour behind schedule. It had sufficient time to reach Swindon 10 minutes before the 7 p.m. Temple Meads to Paddington passenger train.

About 1½ miles east of Wootton Bassett the brick arch in the firebox of the goods engine collapsed. As the engine was not proceeding beyond Swindon, the fire was consequently low and the falling bricks almost put it out. Certainly, steam pressure was so weak that the train came to a standstill.

William Taylor, the head guard, went forward to see what was wrong and F. Merrett, the under guard, was slow in going back down the line placing detonators. In fact, he went only 50 yd instead of the 1,000 yd stipulated in the rule book.

About seven minutes after the goods stopped the head guard returned, climbed into his van, summoned the under guard to join him, and the train left. Travelling at about 7 mph, the goods reached a point 2½ miles west of Swindon when the head guard instructed the under guard to jump out of the van and lay detonators, as the 7 p.m. was due. As soon as the guard got off the passenger train came into sight and he only had time to put down one detonator.

Lt. Col. F.H. Rich, in his report to the Board of Trade, said:

The lights at the tail of the goods train might have been seen by the engine driver of the passenger train for about 700 yards before he reached the goods train; but the passenger train was running at a speed of about 50 miles an hour at the time, the driver had no reason to expect that there was anything on the road. These men have to attend to their engines, and cannot keep their eyes riveted on the road in front of them for every minute of their periods of duty.

If the driver's attention was given to his fire for half a minute prior to the collision, it would be sufficient to have prevented his observing the lights on the goods train. He did not observe them, and was not aware of the train being on the road in front of him, until he ran over the detonating signal, which was subsequently picked up 70 yards from the spot where the collision occurred.

The goods brake van was shattered and seven wagons damaged. *Rob Roy*, a 'Waverley' class 4–4–0 at the head of the passenger train, fell into a field about 45 yd beyond the point of impact and its crew were only slightly injured. Remarkably the four passenger coaches were undamaged and stayed on the rails. Lt Col. Rich commented: 'The block telegraph system is the best known method of preventing such accidents, when strictly adhered to, and used in connexion with the other known means of protection available on railways.' *Rob Roy* was not repaired and was withdrawn in February 1872, the first member of its class to be scrapped, though none were running by the end of 1876. The GWR directors dismissed goods guards Taylor and Merrett for failure to heed regulations.

Ironically, one of Brunel's safety ideas caused an accident at Bathampton on 11 June 1875. The 10.01 a.m. Bristol to Salisbury service, consisting of six coaches and a guard's van hauled by 'Metro' class 2–4–0T No. 970, built in September 1874, failed to take the points at the junction and the locomotive, van and the two leading coaches overturned. One frightened passenger jumped out and was killed when a coach fell on him. Another passenger was fatally injured. The *Bath Chronicle* reported that two men 'with much foresight took with them to the scene of the accident brandy and other stimulants which were found very useful'. Quarrymen and others who visited the scene helped to clear the wreckage.

At Bathampton the Up road to Chippenham was mixed gauge and that to Bradford-on-Avon narrow gauge. So that the road was never wrong for an Up broad-gauge train only one movable point blade was provided, the wheels on the other rail running on their flanges for about 9 ft. The movable blade was the narrow-gauge rail situated on the inside of the curve.

The inquest had its lighter moments. Thomas Baker, an upholsterer said: 'When the train came to a stoppage, I looked out and seeing the carriage before me thrown over, I thought it was time to get out (A laugh).' John Hutton recounted:

When we entered the station I became alarmed at the rate we were going. Four of us were talking, and we saw we were going too fast and laid hold of the seat, knowing that at the rate we were going, the train could not take the points for the branch line. We were travelling at the same rate as the through trains on the main line. I listened to hear whether the engine would take the points and heard the engine strike. I cried out 'She's off the line. I thought it would come to this.' I was in the carriage next to the van: it toppled about and fell over, and I became insensible. When I came to myself I found my right leg out of the window dragging along and the train going on. When it stopped I got out of the carriage by climbing out of the top window.

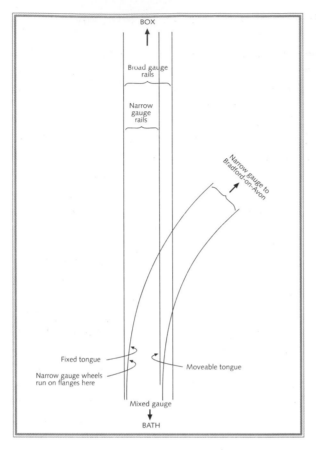

BOX

↑

Broad gauge
rails

Narrow
gauge
rails

Narrow gauge to
Bradford-on-Avon ↗

Fixed tongue

Narrow gauge wheels
run on flanges here

Moveable tongue

Mixed gauge

↓

BATH

Plan of the mixed-gauge junction
at Bathampton.

(*C.G. Maggs*)

The coroner queried: 'I don't exactly understand how your leg could be hanging out of the window?' Witness: 'It was dragging on the ground. I cried out, "Oh, I shall lose my leg", and then put my hand out and pulled it in (Laughter).'

At the inquest it was believed that figures in the signalman's register may have been altered. W. Lewis, a Bath photographer, made a copy, enlarged it ten times, and it was then seen that the record had not been falsified. This was one of the first instances of photography being used for such a purpose.

The Board of Trade inspecting officer, Col. Yolland, believed the accident occurred through the train passing the junction at about 27 mph, a speed which he considered too fast, and recommended a maximum of 10 mph. He wrote that although the fixed point did not 'occasion the accident', the lack of a movable switch inside the outer rail of the curve caused it to occur. He also recommended that double movable switches be installed for both broad- and narrow-gauge lines, and that a length of broad-gauge rail be laid on the branch to provide for possible overrunning of an Up broad-gauge train against signals. Yolland observed that similar junctions at Thingley, and Calne Junction, Chippenham, also needed amending.

There was a poignant moment at the end of the Board of Trade inquiry, held at Bath station, when one of the witnesses, Capt. King, presented Guard Hayter with a 'handsome Bible' inscribed: 'This best of books was presented to George Hayter, a guard in the service of the Great Western Railway, by Edward King, of Seend, Wilts, gentleman, in grateful remembrance in his prompt application of the brake, whereby I was under Divine and overruling Providence preserved from bodily injury at Bathampton on the eleventh day of June 1875.'

An accident did in fact occur at Thingley Junction on 5 November 1875, but the fixed points were not the cause. The 2.30 p.m. Paddington to Temple Meads express, headed by broad-gauge 'Iron Duke' class 4–2–2 *Prometheus*, approached Thingley Junction under clear signals, but just as it reached the Home, it turned red. Driver Edward Price sounded his brake whistle, reversed his engine, but could not stop in time and struck an Up narrow-gauge goods from Salisbury which had passed the branch signals set at danger.

The head guard, Harry Paynter, travelling in the iron-built front brake van, was severely injured, his leg being trapped between a seat and the end of the van. He died next day. The driver of the express was also injured, together with twelve passengers. While they were waiting for a special train to take them to the Bear Hotel, Chippenham, Mr Wright, a commercial traveller, 'opened his samples of wines and spirits and freely distributed them as restoratives for the sufferers'. As bad luck would have it, Reuben Cook of Bath, one of those injured, had also been hurt in the Bathampton accident only five months before.

Driver John Spackman on the goods engine said that he saw the adverse Distant signal and then glanced at the fire. This affected his night sight, and when he looked at the Home signal he believed he saw two white lights (white at this period indicated Clear). He then saw the Down express, reversed his engine and blew the brake whistle.

An almost exact re-enactment of the 1875 accident took place on 16 January 1907. 'Dean Goods' 0–6–0 No. 2448, heading the 5.05 p.m. Swindon to Laira goods, had a clear Down Distant for Thingley Junction. At the junction itself Driver Robert Butt saw to his horror that the 6.30 p.m. Westbury to Chippenham passenger train, hauled by 'River' class 2–4–0 No. 70 *Dart* with four coaches, had run through signals and a

The accident at Thingley Junction, 16 January 1907.

(Author's Collection)

Thingley Junction accident, 16 January 1907: 'River' class 2–4–0 No. 70 *Dart*.

(Author's Collection)

Thingley Junction accident, 16 January 1907: 'Dean Goods' 0–6–0 No. 2448.

(Author's Collection)

collision between the two engines was inevitable. The goods engine was flung on its side across the main line. Nineteen derailed wagons formed two piles each 30 ft high. The first compartment of the leading coach was stoved in by the tender, but had been kept empty as regulations demanded. No passengers in any of the coaches were injured. As both lines were completely blocked, trains were diverted via Badminton until the Down road was cleared by two steam cranes from Swindon the next morning. Both engines were so badly damaged that they had to be cut up on the spot.

Driver Charles Powell of Trowbridge on No. 70 said he missed the Thingley Junction Distant as it was difficult to see from the driver's side. He immediately applied the brake. He intended to stop at the Home signal, but missed that too. His fireman John Sweeney had trouble with the exhaust injector and Powell tried to turn on the live steam injector, which also then failed to work. Powell believed his train had priority over the goods and was expecting his signal to be lowered rather than that for the goods. Col. H.A. Yorke, the Board of Trade inspecting officer, wrote in his report that Signalman Frank Stokes at Thingley Junction would have 'acted with more prudence' had he ensured that the passenger train was stopped before clearing signals for the goods.

The Bathampton area was unfortunate in August 1876. On the 11th a Swindon to Bath broad-gauge goods became divided near Bathampton but the breakaway was not observed until it reached Hampton Row. Then four days later, as the midnight narrow-gauge goods from Bristol to Weymouth was passing Hampton Row, a bale of linen fell from a wagon almost at the rear of the train. This caused another truck laden with six hogsheads of brandy, having a total value of about £550, to derail. One wheel ran on the transoms, some thirty of which were damaged, and the other wheels travelled in the space between the broad and narrow-gauge rails, damaging a considerable number of bolts. With one exception where only one end burst, the violent oscillation caused both ends of each brandy cask to burst, so all the spirit ran to waste.

The driver noticed the wagon off the line and stopped, with the offending vehicle over the Down line. Permanent-way Inspector Evans and packers from Bath appeared with jacks, and by the time the breakdown gang arrived from Bristol the wagon had been rerailed and the line cleared. The train then proceeded, except for the errant truck which was returned to Bath.

On 25 May 1881 another Weymouth goods encountered trouble at Hampton Row. As it passed the level-crossing at about 22 mph, Driver James Furber suddenly realised that Fireman Thomas Simmonds was no longer on the footplate. He stopped the train, called the guard's attention to the missing fireman, and the under guard walked to the rear of the train while Driver Furber and the head guard proceeded on foot to Bathampton station.

Meanwhile, back at Hampton Row, Thomas Pinchin, permanent-way packer, saw a man lying on the embankment 40 to 50 yd from the signal-box. He was alive, but had a large wound over his left eye. Pinchin picked him up; he breathed four or five times and died. His corpse was placed on a trolley and taken to Widcombe police station.

The accident happened because the fireman leaned over to wave to a person by the level-crossing, and in so doing, struck his head on the signal-box. Inspector Liddiard measured the distance from the rails to the box and found it to be 3 ft 11 in. Several tunnel walls were not quite 3 ft from the rails, so this clearance was deemed acceptable.

A similar mishap occurred on 19 October the same year. As the 11 a.m. Bristol to Chippenham passenger train left Box Tunnel, Fireman James Humphries leaned over the side to try to locate a fault with the nearside brake. Unfortunately his head struck one of the Corsham aqueduct's supporting piers and he was knocked off the engine. A platelayer working nearby saw a hat fall and followed the train to pick it up. On reaching the aqueduct he saw Fireman Humphries on the ground with his head bleeding. Although alive, he was unable to speak and died five minutes later. Other platelayers put a trolley on the rails and conveyed the body to Corsham station, where an inquest was held the following day at the Station Hotel. The verdict was 'Accidental death'.

On Saturday 16 September 1893 the 7.55 a.m. Down express from Paddington, consisting of nine coaches, was hauled by 'Achilles' class 2–2–2 No. 3021 *Wigmore Castle*. It slipped a coach at Chippenham and entered Box Tunnel at not more than 44 mph. Driver Charles Haynes said that about ¾ mile from the west end of the tunnel, the right-hand leading wheel seemed to drop outside the right rail with a lurch and loud noise, followed by a second lurch when the driving wheel left the rails. There was then a thud and tremendous lurch and loud noise when the trailing wheels left the road. The engine then jumped about, finally stopping with its right-hand leading wheel over the inside rail of the Up line.

Fireman Gibbons and Locomotive Inspector Bill Greenaway were on the engine, and on hearing an approaching train went to meet it, but they had no light, the gauge lamp being extinguished by the accident. They shouted to the driver of the Up train as it passed about 30 to 40 yd from *Wigmore Castle*.

Driver Thomas Keeling, on 3232 class 2–4–0 No. 3240 with four coaches on the 11.03 a.m. Temple Meads to Chippenham, heard someone on the 6 ft side call 'Stop'. He closed the regulator and was knocked against the front of the firebox and jammed there by coal. Injured and scalded, he freed himself and sent his fireman, Alfred Hales, back to the tunnel mouth to protect his train.

At the Board of Trade Inquiry in November 1893 Keeling recounted:

The tunnel was full of steam and smoke when the accident happened. I was fixed in the wreckage of the engine for about 5 minutes, smothered with flame, smoke and steam. Where I was I never thought I'd get out alive. It seemed to be choking me. I was jammed up against the firebox; everything came off, and the tender was right against us. Hales, my stoker, was stunned for several minutes. Some of the flames were right round our heads. I felt my way about, and, getting away, ultimately found myself between the wheels. I fell down three or four times in my attempt to get away. I have been on the line 39 years, and was never in an accident before.

Mr W. Dickie of Cotham, Bristol, and a friend were in the penultimate coach of the express and gave a graphic description. On realising the train had derailed, they had the presence of mind to lie on the seat and firmly grasp the upholstery. As they lay in the darkness,

Suddenly both of us heard the laboured puffing and hissing of steam from a distance. The sound of it rose above the murmur of voices, and my friend called out to me, 'There's something going to run into us in a minute.' We dared not move, and all we could do in the darkness was to clutch with a firmer grip anything which would help us keep our prone positions on the seats, and listen in the darkness to the rumbling noise of the approaching train and the sound of its jets and puffs of steam, each jerk of which, growing louder, showed us that it was coming nearer and nearer to us, in all probability bringing death in its train. . . . The suspense of those two minutes was terrible. The two minutes seemed an eternity. I cannot tell you what I passed through in that short time. At length came the crash – and we breathed more freely, as we knew that the collision was at the further end, and we were safe.

The train held another passenger with literary ability, S.P. Cochrane, of Newbridge Road, Bath, who wrote:

I occupied a compartment with 5 others, about 4 carriages from the front of the train which was lighted with gas. In what seemed a very short time after entering the tunnel, going at a high rate of speed which was steadily increasing, we experienced a violent shock, and at the same moment the compartment was plunged into total darkness. Someone said, 'Good God, we are off the line', and realising the speed at which we were travelling, our sensations when it became evident that the train had actually left the metals, are impossible to describe. . . . The violent and terrific bumping and jolting over the sleepers threw us first to one side of the carriage and then the other, and must have continued for about 30 seconds before the train came to a standstill. The confusion was heightened by the contents of the luggage racks coming tumbling about our heads.

After this, the first thing we did was to get a light. Matches were struck and newspapers formed into torches, which were lighted, and the windows were opened. . . . Hardly realising the full extent of our danger, we decided to remain in the compartment until some officials came along, but worse was yet to come.

About four minutes after the train had become stationary, to our horror we heard the sound of another train approaching on the up line. . . . The mental terror was agonising in the extreme. The next moment came an awful crash and we were again jolted about most violently. . . . Soon afterwards the guard came along telling all the passengers to make the best of their way towards the rear of the train. . . . By means of fresh newspaper torches we could see that the metals had been torn up and twisted, also the sleepers thrown about . . . there must have been upwards of 100 people gathered together on the line, not knowing which way to turn or what to do. . . . At length we made our way along in the darkness in the best way we could until we met two or three men with lamps, who told us we were 1½ miles from the Corsham end of the tunnel.

The occupants of the train groped their way in single file along the track. I joined a party of 15 or 20, and eventually we secured the services of a man and a lamp, thus rendering the remainder of our progress relatively easy.

On reaching Corsham a train was waiting which took most of the passengers of the express back to Chippenham, where the 'Dutchman' was stopped for the purpose of taking on the West of England passengers via Trowbridge and Limpley Stoke. We arrived at Bath at 3 o'clock. I should like to add that when the officials arrived on the scene they were most anxious to do everything they could to allay alarm or contribute towards the better convenience of the passengers.

Signalman Bow at Box Station East raised the alarm when the express did not appear and telegraphed to Box Tunnel East box to stop all Down trains. About ten minutes later Bow saw Woodward, guard of the Up train, and Locomotive Inspector Greenaway running to his box. So many messages had to be sent from Box that the signal-box could not cope and the telegraph at Box post office was also used. Within a few minutes of the Royal United Hospital at Bath receiving news of the accident, beds were ready for a large number of patients, but fortunately only seven needed to be admitted.

Driver Wiltshire of Box went on foot into the tunnel, and he and men from the Bath stone wharves and permanent-way men working half a mile away aided passengers from the coaches. The worst injured were placed in the undamaged last coach of the Up train and taken to Bath.

Breakdown gangs were sent from Bath, Bristol, Trowbridge and Swindon, a total of 250 men being employed to clear the line. No. 3021 and No. 3240 were so tightly jammed that two other engines failed to draw them apart, so a further two were telegraphed for. On Sunday morning the engines were extricated, followed at long intervals during the day by coaches. Naphtha lights were used for illumination and two vans placed on the Up line for labourers' sleeping accommodation.

Track repairs were facilitated by the fact that longitudinal baulks with rail still attached, which had been replaced by a new cross-sleeper road, were still awaiting removal, so the baulks and rail were temporarily re-laid, saving the additional hours which would have been necessary had new material needed to be brought in.

The first train through the tunnel after the accident was a heavily laden excursion from Paddington to Weston-super-Mare composed of seventeen bogie coaches plus three guard's vans. It passed through at 4 a.m. very slowly.

No. 3021 *Wigmore Castle* had been built at Swindon in April 1891 as a broad-gauge convertible and named after the Welsh seat of the late Sir Charles Alexander Wood, for many years deputy chairman of the GWR.

While No. 3021 was undergoing repair, its frames were lengthened at the front end to accommodate a bogie, thus giving a steadier and safer ride. By December 1894 all members of the 'Achilles' class had been similarly converted. No. 3240 had been built in November 1892.

Early on 15 November 1912 the 11.45 p.m. goods ex-Chippenham, consisting of forty-three wagons and a brake van, emerged from Box Tunnel at about 12.10 a.m. when Midland Railway wagon No. 1452, about two-thirds of the way along the train, was derailed at the site of the later Mill Lane Halt. The trouble was caused by a brake block from Rhymney Iron Company's wagon No. 2105 getting under a wheel of the MR wagon. The Midland wagon drew several more off the track. They ran derailed through Middle Hill Tunnel, but points at Box station caused them to overturn. Goods Guard J. Bunning of Chippenham applied his brake hard and kept his own van and the wagons ahead of it from derailing. As the gradient from Box to Bathampton is 1 in 850 down, the load was not missed and it was only when the driver looked back at Bathampton that he saw he had only fourteen wagons.

As Box station was closed for the night the stationmaster and his staff were roused and on duty by 12.30 a.m. Fifty men cleared the wreckage below the road bridge carrying what is now the A4. One of William Butler's tar wagons was also involved in the derailment and leaked tar over the track.

An accident occurred on 29 January 1940 at Hay Lane, but owing to wartime secrecy details were restricted. Ice in that severe winter had brought down the block instrument wire between Hay Lane and Wootton Bassett, so a 20-minute time-interval working was introduced. Frozen points at Swindon were causing problems, and at about 3.50 a.m. no fewer than four trains stood head-to-tail at Hay Lane box awaiting clearance to the next box, Rushey Platt. The fourth train was the 9.16 p.m. Plymouth to Paddington Postal comprising 'Castle' class 4–6–0 No. 5026 *Criccieth Castle* and six vans.

After waiting the requisite 20 minutes the 10 a.m. special freight from Severn Tunnel Junction to Old Oak Common, consisting of 28XX class 2–8–0 No. 2868, thirty-four coal wagons and a brake van, left Wootton Bassett East. Although the driver proceeded cautiously it was not until he was 20 yd away that he spotted the red lamp waved by the Postal's guard. He closed the regulator, applied the brake and worked the sand lever, then he and his fireman jumped from the engine before an impact at about 5 mph.

The rear stowage van was forced through the vehicle in front, and of the twenty-five post office employees eighteen were injured, while one van was completely destroyed

4–6–0 No. 6910 *Gossington Hall* overturned at Wootton Bassett Junction on 27 June 1946
when hauling the 11.50 p.m. Paddington–Carmarthen goods.

(Author's Collection)

and another seriously damaged. The Postal was driven forward and struck the train ahead
– the 4.45 p.m. Penzance to Paddington passenger – but this only received superficial
damage to the 'tail traffic' of milk tanks.

The guard of the train from Severn Tunnel Junction correctly ran back to protect the
rear of his train, and about ¾ mile from his van saw the 12.40 a.m. Westbury to Oxley
goods approaching through the snow. He placed three detonators on the line, waved his
red lamp and the train stopped in good time. The guard of the 12.40 a.m. from
Westbury similarly protected his train, successfully stopping the 9.45 p.m. Penzance to
Paddington express passenger. There were now seven trains in the 1½ miles west of Hay
Lane signal-box!

Because the Postal blocked the Down line the fireman of the third train in the queue –
the 4.45 p.m. Penzance to Paddington passenger – went forward with detonators to
protect Down trains. Signalman Albert Fry in Hay Lane box, suspecting something was
wrong by the noise and lights in the distance, had already sent six bells, 'Obstruction –
Danger', to Rushey Platt box. Frozen points at Swindon hampered the despatch of
breakdown vans and it was about twelve hours before the line could be cleared.

The last accident of any consequence on the line occurred at Wootton Bassett on
27 June 1946. 'Hall' class 4–6–0 No. 6910 *Gossington Hall* overturned, blocking the
junction, while working the 11.50 p.m. Paddington to Carmarthen goods. Twenty-three
wagons telescoped, completely blocking both the Bath and Badminton lines.

Chapter Eight

RAILWAYS ASSOCIATED WITH THE SWINDON TO BATH LINE

SWINDON TO GLOUCESTER

Immediately west of Swindon Junction, the Gloucester line swings away to the north-west. It was built by the broad-gauge Cheltenham & Great Western Union Railway and opened to Cirencester on 31 May 1841. Like the Swindon to Bath line, it suffered from slipping embankments.

The extension from Kemble to Gloucester had several major engineering features, including the 1,864-yd-long Sapperton Tunnel and seven viaducts. The line opened to Gloucester on 12 May 1845.

The section of line through the Stroud Valley was well known during the first half of the twentieth century for its extensive steam railmotor and auto-train services. The opening of halts between main stations encouraged more people to use trains, while a conductor on the train selling tickets meant that the expense of manning halts was avoided.

The Swindon to Gloucester line was the GWR's main line to South Wales until after the opening of the Severn Tunnel to passenger trains in 1886, and even after opening remained an alternative route when the tunnel closed for maintenance.

CHELTENHAM, SWINDON, ANDOVER AND SOUTHAMPTON

At Rushey Platt Junction, 1¼ miles west of Swindon Junction, the Swindon, Marlborough & Andover Railway curved southwards to Swindon Town station. Swindon to Marlborough opened on 27 July 1881 and through to Andover and Southampton on 5 February 1883. An extension northwards to Cirencester opened on 18 December 1883, crossing the GWR at Rushey Platt. The line, by then known as the Midland & South Western Junction Railway, eventually reached Andoversford and Cheltenham, with through trains running from the Midland Railway's Lansdown station to Southampton from 1 August 1891.

The line was particularly valuable during both world wars, taking troops and supplies to the south coast and returning with ambulance trains. Milk traffic was also an important commodity with four vans starting from Cricklade each evening and the train arriving at Andover with seventeen. Here a London & South Western Railway engine and guard were scheduled to take them onwards to Clapham Junction and Waterloo.

The MSWJR was an independent company, but was absorbed by the GWR in 1923. Arguably the line may have enjoyed a better service had it been run jointly by the LMS and SR. With the development of road transport the line became uneconomic and

Swindon Junction, *c.* 1890. The Gloucester line curves right and the
broad-gauge engine shed is the last building on the left.

(Author's Collection)

A Swindon Town–Cheltenham stopping train passes Rushey Platt Junction, *c.* 1930,
and will shortly cross the GWR Swindon Junction–Wootton Bassett line.
The engine is an ex-Midland & South Western Junction Railway 0–6–0 reboilered by the GWR.

(P.Q. Treloar Collection)

A view taken on 21 April 1965 of the MSWJR bridge over the
Swindon Junction–Wootton Bassett line, left; the curve from Swindon Junction to Swindon Town,
right; and the 'Dump' beyond Rushey Platt Junction signal-box.

(C.G. Maggs)

passenger services were withdrawn on 11 September 1961, when much of the line closed. The section from Rushey Platt to Cirencester was cut back to the electricity sidings at Moredon on 11 April 1964 and this spur closed completely in 1973. The section from Rushey Platt to Swindon Town enjoyed a brief new surge of life when it carried material for constructing the M4, but this length closed in October 1970. The Swindon & Cricklade Railway Society has a centre at Blunsdon and members have re-laid track along part of the MSWJR's formation.

WOOTTON BASSETT TO FILTON JUNCTION

During the latter half of the nineteenth century people often jokingly said that the initials GWR stood for 'Great Way Round', and certainly many of its main lines were far from being direct. When the Severn Tunnel was opened trains from London to South Wales had to curve southwards at Wootton Bassett, pass through Bath and Bristol, and then bear northwards again to reach the tunnel. Trains were travelling an unnecessary 10 miles and a direct link was needed through the southern end of the Cotswolds between Wootton Bassett and Filton, north of Bristol. Coupled with the criticism of indirectness was the fact that many people in South Wales were very dissatisfied with the service provided by the GWR, and they threatened to build an entirely new railway from Cardiff to Andover, from where trains could run over the LSWR to London. (It is interesting to note that the Carmarthen–Waterloo DMU service introduced on 30 May 1994 was almost a fulfilment of these wishes.)

The GWR countered this threat to its South Wales traffic by proposing the Bristol & South Wales Direct Railway. This 30-mile-long line from Wootton Bassett to Filton Junction had several advantages. In addition to shortening the distance from Wales to London it avoided two steep inclines, enabling engines to pull double their previous loads, and also provided an alternative route between London and Bristol. The BSWDR also provided a more direct route to Avonmouth, where a new dock was being built. A further advantage was that it would reduce the number of trains on the Bristol to Bathampton section, over which traffic had increased since the opening of the Severn Tunnel, and which could not be easily quadrupled because of the expense of widening the many tunnels, cuttings, embankments and viaducts.

The BSWDR undertaking was the biggest of its kind to be carried out since the extension of the Great Central Railway to London a few years before. It was laid for speedy running, with no gradient steeper than 1 in 300 and no curve sharper than a 1 mile radius. Considering that the line had to cross the Cotswolds this was a fine achievement. Four of the stations had quadruple track, enabling non-stop trains to bypass the platforms and, if necessary, overtake slower ones. Most of the embankments were wide enough for quadrupling throughout.

The first section of the line to be opened was from Wootton Bassett to Badminton on 1 January 1903, but this was only for goods traffic. The first through goods train to use the line left Bristol on 1 May 1903 and the first passenger train operated on 1 July 1903. Four new direct expresses from Paddington to South Wales ran over the new line.

The former Malmesbury branch bay platform at Dauntsey, 23 August 1955.
The Malmesbury branch curved to the right of the signal-box.

(C.G. Maggs)

The Bristol & South Wales Direct Railway crosses the Malmesbury branch west of Little Somerford.
A view towards Malmesbury, 23 August 1955.

(C.G. Maggs)

An 0–6–0PT pushes the 5.35 p.m. Calne–Westbury auto-train past Chippenham East inner Home signal
in 1953. Behind the engine is a Harris-branded van, while the engine shed stands on the left.

(Roy Ball)

DAUNTSEY TO MALMESBURY

The Malmesbury branch was unique in that during its lifetime it changed its junction from one main line to another of equal importance. The single-line branch from Dauntsey to Malmesbury opened on 17 December 1877 and trouble was encountered during the first week, with a train crashing through the unopened crossing gates at Dauntsey Road. Apparently the crossing keeper was unable to get out of his cottage in time because a door handle came off!

When the BSWDR was under construction a temporary connection was laid near Little Somerford for carrying materials to the new line. Some thirty years later, as an economy measure, it was decided that a permanent connection would be laid from Little Somerford station on the BSWDR to the Malmesbury branch at Kingsmead Crossing, so that most of the branch towards Dauntsey could be abandoned. These alterations came into use on 17 July 1933.

With increasing road competition, passenger services ended on 8 September 1951, but the substantial goods traffic continued, trains sometimes consisting of thirty wagons. Reduced traffic did not cause the withdrawal of freight services. Instead, the reason given by BR for closure on 11 November 1962 was the expense of repairing collapsing culverts.

CHIPPENHAM TO CALNE

The Calne branch was built by the Calne Railway to serve sixteen mills and the largest bacon factory in England. The line opened to freight on 29 October 1862 and to passengers on 3 November. Although in its first month the line was well used, unfortunately the company's debts were so great that they proved impossible to repay, so the line was sold to the GWR on 1 July 1892.

In about 1900 it was proposed to extend the branch to Marlborough and join the MSWJR's Swindon to Andover line, but the project was modified to the far cheaper option of a railway bus service between Calne and Marlborough. Starting on 10 October 1904, it was one of the earliest motorbus services in the country.

To avoid locomotives having to run round at Calne and Chippenham, use was made of either steam railcars or auto-trains. The Calne branch was unusual for a 5¼ mile-long line in that it was worked by engines from no fewer than four depots – Bath, Bristol, Chippenham and Westbury. Officially speed was restricted to a maximum of 30 mph, though one Bath engine reached Chippenham signal-box from Calne in 7½ minutes, giving an average speed of 43 mph.

Black Dog was a particularly interesting station. It was opened in 1875 as a private station for the Marquess of Lansdowne, though the public was allowed to use it. The marquess paid part of the stationmaster's wages and provided him with a house and 4 tons of coal annually. It did not become a public station until 15 September 1952, its first name-board being erected just before Christmas. Until that year the halt did not exist for ticketing purposes, passengers booking to Calne or Stanley Bridge.

Messrs Harris sent bacon and pork products from Calne in large quantities, conveyed in dedicated vans with special enamel plates announcing the name of the manufacturer and its destination.

The branch was especially busy during the Second World War, when 20,000 servicemen were stationed in the area, but owing to road competition, freight services

The fireman of the Calne train collects the token at Chippenham East signal-box, *c.* 1962.

(Christopher Kent)

The 12.28 p.m. ex–Bristol Temple Meads approaching Calne hauled by 4575 class 2–6–2T No. 5511, *c.* 1938. Note the Calne–Manchester 'Siphon' van at the rear of the train.

(E.J.M. Hayward)

were withdrawn in 1963 and, as the average branch train carried only thirteen passengers, the line closed completely on 18 September 1965.

THINGLEY JUNCTION TO TROWBRIDGE AND WESTBURY

On 5 September 1848 the first section of the single broad-gauge Wilts, Somerset & Weymouth Railway opened between Thingley Junction and Westbury. Brunel, the line's engineer, had strong objections to facing points, especially away from stations where speed might be high, so at Thingley Junction trains had to stop and reverse into a siding before they could proceed to Melksham. The line eventually reached Salisbury on 30 June 1856 and Weymouth on 20 January 1857. The WSWR was converted to narrow gauge in June 1874, the first in the area to be altered. Traffic grew to such an extent that the Weymouth line was doubled in the 1880s and the Salisbury branch between 1896 and 1901.

The opening of the Patney & Chirton to Westbury line on 1 October 1900 meant that Weymouth trains could use a shorter route and so traffic through Melksham decreased. Because the line connected the Bristol to Reading, and Westbury to Reading lines, it

A War Department class 2–8–0 carrying a 'perishable' headcode, at Thingley Junction, *c.* 1952,
with a train from Trowbridge. Notice the water tower for the locomotive supply.

(T.J. Saunders)

Thingley Junction from the cab of a DMU working the 17.34 Swindon–Warminster service, 13 June 1988.

(C.G. Maggs)

Bathampton, 10 April 2002. A rear view of No. 150253
working the 12.30 Cardiff–Portsmouth Harbour train, taking the curve to Westbury.

(C.G. Maggs)

No. 6000 *King George V*, now preserved at the Steam Museum of the Great Western Railway,
rounding the curve at Bathampton, *c.* 1960, with the 7.15 a.m. Plymouth–Paddington (Sundays),
having been diverted via Bradford-on-Avon and Melksham, probably because of work on Box Tunnel.
The goods and engineer's sidings are on the right.

(Russell Leitch)

proved useful as an alternative route in the event of one becoming blocked, while the opening on 10 March 1895 of the North loop at Bradford Junction had already offered an alternative route between Bathampton and Chippenham. The local passenger service from Chippenham to Trowbridge was withdrawn on 18 April 1966, and the intermediate stations closed. The line was singled on 26 February 1967. However, increased road congestion has resulted in a passenger service being reintroduced, and Melksham station was reopened on 13 May 1985.

BATHAMPTON TO TROWBRIDGE & WESTBURY

Initially, the Thingley to Trowbridge section of the WSWR was rightly considered more important than the Bathampton to Trowbridge section as it offered a better connection to London, owing to developing traffic over the route between South Wales, Bristol and Salisbury, Southampton and Portsmouth. However, the Bathampton to Trowbridge section has increased greatly in importance.

Bathampton to Trowbridge was not opened until 2 February 1857. Although the station at Bradford-on-Avon had been completed in 1848, a shortage of cash had prevented the rails from being laid! The single broad-gauge line was converted to narrow gauge in June 1874. Following the opening of the Severn Tunnel in 1886, and with the development of Southampton, it formed the most direct route for coal from South Wales destined for ships' bunkers at Southampton and Portsmouth. Traffic increased to such an extent that Bathampton to Bradford-on-Avon was doubled on 17 May 1885.

Passenger traffic between South Wales, Bristol and Portsmouth has grown so that nowadays for much of the day there is an hourly service, plus an approximately two-hourly service from Bristol to Weymouth. An interesting introduction since privatisation is a through service between Temple Meads and Waterloo, providing competition with the First Great Western service to Paddington.

Appendix 1

Corsham Signalman

Norman Whalley

What was it like being a signalman at Corsham? I was there from 1948 till March 1965, when I moved to Thingley Junction. Corsham box had the advantage over many boxes in that it had electric light, running water, a flush toilet rather than an Elsan, and was in a sheltered position facing south. Signal-boxes with so much glass suffered extremes of temperature.

The direction a box faced affected its temperature. If a box, such as Thingley Junction, faced north, this meant that the slots at the base of the outside wall for the point rodding to pass through also faced north and allowed a cold north wind to whistle up through the slots in the lever frame. A crafty signalman covered these with newspaper, but the draught could be so strong that it blew the paper away. Corsham box faced south, so the rodding slots also faced south. It had the additional advantage that the cutting sheltered it from north winds.

A couple of permanent-way men unloaded coal once a year for the open-grate fire, replaced in about 1960 by a coal-burning stove. They never delivered enough coal and when the opportunity arose I begged a large lump from a tender engine and broke it up with the aid of a fireman's big coal hammer which the box inherited. I didn't like asking for coal from the tank engine working the 'tripper' as it had little to spare.

I used to like the night shift the best and drank coffee to keep me awake. I boiled the kettle on a gas ring. Not so many trains ran at night as during the day and sometimes there was a gap as long as 1½ hours when I could read undisturbed. Working at night, with Box Tunnel not far away, enabled me to identify with my fictitious colleague in Charles Dickens's short story *The Signalman*. Corsham box was certainly rather spooky.

One of the night goods trains was the 4.05 p.m. from Exeter which reached Corsham between 3 and 4 a.m. In the 1950s it was often headed by an 'Austerity' 2–8–0 and often I opened a window, put my megaphone to my ear and listened to its progress up through the tunnel. Sometimes the slow 'Clump, clump, clump' stopped and shortly after, the very loud alarm bell would ring.

I got on to Control and they either sent an engine from Bristol, or any light engine available in the area, or perhaps even an engine from a goods train waiting in Bathampton loop. The banker was not coupled and dropped off at the aqueduct. One memorable week the 4.05 stopped four times!

Once I experienced a runaway. The Down goods from Chippenham arrived at Corsham one afternoon. The guard cut off his van and a couple of wagons and left them on the main line while the engine and rest of the train shunted into the yard.

Porter Norman Whalley, right, outside Corsham goods shed, May 1948. He is dressed in army uniform and GWR cap. Owing to the postwar cloth shortage, no uniform was available. On the left is porter Gilbert Gardner. *(Norman Whalley Collection)*

Signalman Norman Whalley hands the token to the driver of diesel–hydraulic D7025 at Thingley Junction, August 1967.

(Norman Whalley Collection)

I noticed a movement, and there was the van and wagons running back down the 1 in 660 towards Thingley. I could hardly believe it! I saw the track circuit flick on as they passed the outer Home signal. I 'blocked back' and sent 'train running away on the wrong line' to Thingley Junction. The driver, authorised to reverse, caught the runaways about halfway to Thingley.

Another exciting moment was when I received seven bells (Stop and Examine Train) from Thingley Junction. When it arrived I put it into one of the Down sidings, saw flames leaping up and immediately sent for the fire brigade. They soon arrived and from the access road near Potley Bridge squirted water on to the fire and quickly put it out.

1964 was a year of Beatlemania. The Beatles had filmed *A Hard Day's Night* on a train at South Molton. News soon spread round Corsham that that very train with the Beatles on board would actually be passing through the station. Literally hundreds gathered at the lineside to see it pass. This it did at high speed and, unfortunately for the spectators, the Beatles didn't look out and wave.

Several trains were given nicknames. The 9.50 p.m. passenger train from Paddington was 'The Owl', the 4.20 a.m. off Bath 'The Waker', while the Up fully fitted train from Fry's, Keynsham, was 'The Cocoa'.

Fog was a nuisance. Two hundred yards away was my marker point – the Up Main Starting signal – and when I couldn't see it, I called out the permanent-way men for fog duty. One was placed at the Down Distant signal and Up and Down Main signals to lay a detonator if at Danger. No fogman was needed for the Distant signal in Box Tunnel. As there was a siding between the signal-box and the main line, a groundman was required to check that each train had a tail lamp. After fogging, ganger Harry Stanley brought in a fogman sheet for me to sign.

Freezing weather brought problems. Various bearings on a signal could freeze and make it inoperable. To free it I had to get some cotton waste, put paraffin on it, press the waste round the bearing, light a match and, hey presto, the bearing was free.

One great advantage of being a signalman was that you were pretty much your own boss. The Corsham stationmaster visited the box every weekday to sign the register, but generally didn't interfere. The signalling inspector from Bristol looked in about once a year, and he, too, signed the book. Perhaps most important of all, I had a good wife willing to adapt to my irregular mealtimes, as I could be on 6 a.m.–2 p.m., 2–10 p.m., or 10 p.m.–6 a.m., and on Sundays 9 p.m.–2 a.m. Monday.

Appendix 2

Box & Bathampton Stationmaster

Wilf Talbot

Each morning in the early 1960s I arrived at Box station at about 8–8.30 a.m. and greeted the staff – a junior clerk and a porter. First I attended to correspondence, such as from the Divisional Office and from other stations. Various notices were received from the Divisional Office appertaining to the running of trains. I took these to the signalman and conferred with him as to the satisfactory working of trains, etc.

I inspected the station premises to see that everything was clean and tidy and that the notice boards had up-to-date notices.

I inspected the goods yard to see that there was no delay in unloading goods and coal from wagons.

As I lived at Bathampton, after lunch I visited Bathampton station and conferred with the porter-in-charge as to any problems, etc., occurring, and to see that the station was clean and tidy. I went to the goods yard to check that all was well, and visited the timber yard and conferred with the management staff in regard to their traffic on the private siding. Generally it was timber and tree trunks in, with nothing despatched by rail.

I then returned to Box station and visited the signal-box to see the afternoon signalman.

Later on I went to Mill Lane Halt, manned 8 a.m.–5 p.m. by a porter, collected the cash and returned to Box station.

Details of all train tickets issued were recorded and the cash checked, as were the details of parcels forwarded and the cash paid for their carriage. All cash was then placed in the safe for sending to Bristol the next day.

I attended to any further correspondence and returned home about 5 p.m.

Once I acted as pilot through Box Tunnel when single-line working was introduced for part of the Up road to be re-laid. To ensure safety, the rule book required stringent precautions. In Box signal-box I completed the pilotman's forms. One was given to the signalman, who signed for it, I kept another and the third was given to the district inspector in overall charge. I wore a red armlet with 'Pilotman' in white letters.

Accompanied by the district inspector, I got on an engine and travelled on the Up road to Corsham, where I presented a form to the signalman and stationmaster there. The Up road between Box and Corsham was now declared closed and handed to the permanent-way department. All points which had become facing points were required to be clipped and locked.

I explained to the driver of a Down train stopped at Corsham that single-line working was in force, showed him my form and rode with him to Box station. At Box station an Up train was stopped, explanations made; it reversed back over the crossover to the Down road and then proceeded 'wrong line' to Corsham, where it regained the correct road. This procedure was repeated until the engineering department had finished work on the Up road and normal working could be resumed.

Stationmaster Wilf Talbot on the Down platform at Bathampton, 1964.

(W. Talbot Collection)

Appendix 3

Refuge Sidings & Running Loops for Freight Trains

Station	Up Refuge Siding	Up Running Loop	No. of wagons in addition to engine and van	Down Refuge Siding	Down Running Loop	No. of wagons in addition to engine and van
Hay Lane	–	1	118	–	1	118
Wootton Bassett	1	–	57	1	–	43
Wootton Bassett	–	1	74	–	1	57
Wootton Bassett						
Incline s.b.	1	–	43	1	–	57
Dauntsey	1	–	44	1	–	57
Langley Crossing s.b.	1	–	58	1	–	43
Chippenham	1	–	44	–	–	–
Thingley Jct. s.b.	1		51	–	–	–
Thingley Jct. s.b.	–	1*	75	–	1*	75
Thingley West s.b.	–	1	60	–	1	60
Box	–	–	–	1	–	57
Bathampton	1	–	42	–	–	–
Bathampton West s.b.	–	1	65	–	1	145

* Up or Down Loop on Up side

Corsham station, 1878.

APPENDIX 4

MISCELLANEOUS

Annual Coal Tonnage 1962

Chippenham	14,403
Corsham	3,118
Dauntsey	886
Wootton Bassett	833

Maximum loading of Up Passenger Trains through Box Tunnel, 1911

Passenger Trains with one Engine	No. of wheels
3001 class 4–2–2	72
Side tank passenger engines	72
806 class 2–4–0	80
Other large passenger engines	96

Goods Trains

	No. of wagons		
Trains assisted up incline	Coal	Goods	Empties
2–8–0	63	90	100
2–6–0	50	70	80
Ordinary tender and tank engines	40	50	60

APPENDIX 5

STATION ACCOMMODATION, 1956

Station		Crane tons cwt	
Wootton Bassett	GPFLHC	1	10
Dauntsey	GPFLHC	–	–
Christian Malford Halt	P*	–	–
Chippenham	GPFLHC	6	00
Corsham	GP	2	00
Box Mill Lane Platform	P	–	–
Box	GPFLHC	6	00
Bathford Halt	P*	–	–
Bathampton	GP	–	–

Key

G   Goods traffic

P   Passenger, parcels and miscellaneous traffic

P*   Passenger, but not parcels or miscellaneous traffic

F   End loading dock for furniture vans, carriages, motor cars, portable engines and machines on wheels (i.e. by goods train)

L   Livestock

H   Horseboxes and prize cattle vans

C   Carriages and motor cars by passenger or parcels train

STATION	YEAR	STAFF		TOTAL RECEIPTS	PASSENGER TRAIN TRAFFIC						
		Supervisory and Wages (all Grades)	Paybill Expenses		Tickets issued	Season Tickets	Receipts				
							Passengers (including Season Tickets, etc.)	Parcels	Miscellaneous	Total	
		No.	£	£	No.	No.	£	£	£	£	
Swindon Jct. Passenger	1903	168	15,803	42,398	260,276	*	31,494	5,078	5,826	42,398	
	1913	202	16,668	45,496	279,612	*	36,870	4,477	4,149	45,496	
	1923	257	46,308	79,153	290,890	341	66,790	7,550	4,813	79,153	
	1924	257	47,577	86,922	323,460	341	74,819	7,702	4,401	86,922	
	1925	249	47,370	93,677	335,629	368	77,824	10,906	4,947	93,677	
	1926	249	44,358	82,644	283,163	288	68,110	9,626	4,908	82,644	
	1927	256	47,323	88,964	293,504	315	72,958	10,727	5,279	88,964	
	1928	§255	§47,699	89,269	297,180	365	73,032	10,845	5,392	89,269	
	1929	§254	§46,973	91,138	302,803	338	73,600	11,633	5,905	91,138	
	1930	§251	§47,301	90,783	283,593	327	72,005	12,193	6,585	90,783	
	1931	§250	§45,261	83,569	252,143	261	65,441	11,646	6,482	83,569	
	1932	§245	§43,204	76,714	235,198	259	59,934	10,993	5,787	76,714	
	1933	§239	§42,315	74,916	226,110	208	58,126	11,349	5,441	74,916	
Swindon Jct. Goods	1903	*	*	62,525							
	1913	*	2,221	77,484							
	1923	56	9,157	183,335							
	1924	79	11,538	185,889							
	1925	78	12,386	180,344							
	1926	70	11,770	152,515							
	1927	71	11,792	184,538							
	1928	73	12,847	201,923							
	1929	75	13,737	193,524							
	1930	81	13,161	207,106							
	1931	71	12,389	180,104							
	1932	70	11,738	147,668							
	1933	74	12,385	148,452							
Wootton Bassett	1903	22	1,463	16,378	55,263	*	2,323	488	5,553	8,364	
	1913	19	1,497	16,187	47,131	*	2,274	443	6,913	9,630	
	1923	22	3,808	27,523	38,872	599	3,127	578	13,149	16,854	
	1924	22	3,699	24,868	41,434	690	3,272	578	11,317	15,167	
	1925	22	3,766	24,815	44,124	825	3,454	598	11,268	15,320	
	1926	22	3,601	24,064	42,753	752	3,194	575	11,334	15,103	
	1927	22	3,650	27,835	46,693	711	3,283	548	11,622	15,453	
	1928	22	3,620	26,748	45,157	781	3,075	552	14,282	17,909	
	1929	22	3,504	26,191	42,580	792	3,044	532	15,036	18,612	
	1930	22	3,514	24,308	42,000	792	2,865	365	13,720	16,950	
	1931	21	3,417	27,502	40,617	717	2,518	356	15,648	18,522	
	1932	21	3,226	33,587	37,415	665	2,420	274	24,234	26,928	
	1933	20	3,223	41,828	32,112	611	2,177	292	32,731	35,200	
Dauntsey	1903	11	661	7,145	15,028	*	1,186	278	3,425	4,889	
	1913	10	735	6,258	13,868	*	1,051	120	2,804	3,975	
	1923	12	1,705	16,191	16,750	46	1,622	344	9,661	11,627	
	1924	12	1,811	14,329	15,910	67	1,649	332	8,016	9,997	
	1925	12	1,876	14,549	15,347	62	1,572	342	8,342	10,256	
	1926	12	1,882	13,118	13,343	52	1,313	270	7,764	9,347	
	1927	12	1,928	12,642	14,221	66	1,347	202	6,175	7,724	
	1928	9	1,894	8,583	18,665	67	1,525	165	2,904	4,594	
	1929	9	1,845	7,018	12,831	73	1,276	146	2,394	3,816	
	1930	9	1,824	6,025	11,325	93	1,182	155	1,997	3,334	
	1931	11	1,627	6,066	12,907	59	1,061	133	2,098	3,292	
	1932	10	1,480	4,199	11,815	44	944	117	1,392	2,453	
	1933	7	1,318	3,486	8,211	57	783	132	926	1,841	
Christian Malford Halt	Opened October, 1926										
	1926			66	1,628	—	66	—	—	66	
	1927			413	8,732	16	413	—	—	413	
	1928			490	9,104	12	490	—	—	490	
	1929			486	8,866	16	486	—	—	486	
	1930	Included with Chippenham		514	9,402	12	514	—	—	514	
	1931			383	7,553	12	383	—	—	383	
	1932			349	7,111	15	349	—	—	349	
	1933			331	6,528	16	331	—	—	331	

* Not available   §Including Telegraph Staff and Expenses from 1928

GOODS TRAIN TRAFFIC										
Forwarded			Received			Coal and Coke 'Not Charged' (Forwarded and Received)	Total Goods Tonnage	Total Receipts (excluding 'Not Charged' Coal and Coke)	Livestock (Forwarded and Received)	Total Carted Tonnage (included in Total Goods Tonnage)
Coal and Coke 'Charged'	Other Minerals	General Merchandise	Coal and Coke 'Charged'	Other Minerals	General Merchandise					
Tons	Tons	Tons	Tons	Tons	Tons	Tons	Tons	£	Wagons	Tons
1,423	1,720	12,068	11,684	16,900	63,517	18,256	125,568	62,525	755	26,043
387	3,580	15,403	7,584	15,122	77,030	29,057	148,163	77,484	987	29,837
1,796	29,106	23,961	1,797	32,925	80,522	51,481	221,588	183,335	574	40,005
977	17,149	18,694	2,547	28,770	110,178	63,621	241,936	185,889	360	41,642
2,031	13,370	25,609	1,419	32,397	98,584	57,995	231,405	180,344	686	43,195
918	10,932	17,798	4,954	28,388	87,499	40,480	190,969	152,515	450	42,148
447	17,427	18,607	1,736	28,052	103,708	80,490	250,467	184,538	299	46,298
1,369	17,680	20,252	2,561	35,670	113,915	97,702	289,649	201,923	727	44,620
2,477	9,433	23,020	2,174	31,126	112,749	101,603	282,582	193,524	636	47,382
3,205	7,906	22,457	3,199	37,195	128,969	89,977	292,908	207,106	873	44,849
1,830	7,627	19,280	4,046	43,475	116,187	88,714	281,159	180,104	740	40,486
1,679	7,319	18,962	3,951	22,218	96,953	87,705	238,787	147,668	399	40,745
2,435	7,725	19,742	4,062	25,528	97,227	83,957	240,676	148,452	424	47,286
8	107	4,172	2,868	4,433	7,498	2,726	21,812	8,014	182	2,263
16	67	3,327	2,559	4,905	5,218	2,359	18,451	6,557	155	1,935
−	133	3,729	2,769	4,595	4,070	3,428	18,724	10,669	272	1,551
−	151	2,672	1,968	4,057	4,594	3,749	17,191	9,701	233	2,080
32	102	2,855	2,158	3,367	4,477	4,081	17,072	9,495	255	1,559
38	71	1,940	2,363	3,707	4,771	2,964	15,854	8,961	240	1,555
−	168	2,601	1,629	10,942	4,963	4,855	25,158	12,382	184	1,500
−	103	2,140	747	4,760	4,389	5,457	17,596	8,839	277	1,273
22	94	1,451	757	1,965	4,272	5,541	14,102	7,579	259	1,166
29	268	1,502	818	3,206	3,963	7,089	16,875	7,358	246	1,099
34	174	2,526	556	1,975	4,662	8,530	18,457	8,980	170	1,228
−	176	933	441	1,380	5,295	6,573	14,708	6,659	135	1,372
−	415	1,387	234	2,618	4,734	6,903	16,291	6,628	140	2,262
8	−	569	1,497	2,757	1,941	398	7,170	2,256	160	383
−	−	855	1,711	2,622	2,040	504	7,732	2,283	335	292
−	−	1,377	1,704	2,386	2,294	1,084	8,845	4,564	77	357
22	9	1,232	2,103	2,595	2,330	1,036	9,327	4,332	55	383
−	−	1,193	2,037	3,059	2,249	1,152	9,690	4,293	44	328
40	−	1,078	1,144	2,771	2,156	822	8,011	3,771	64	318
20	25	948	1,727	2,509	3,012	1,334	9,575	4,918	42	325
−	202	1,157	1,382	2,434	1,943	1,183	8,301	3,989	42	205
−	−	873	1,414	1,589	1,768	1,070	6,714	3,302	28	197
24	−	783	1,353	763	1,447	1,146	5,516	2,691	53	186
−	−	627	1,442	626	1,825	1,194	5,714	2,774	34	162
−	−	314	1,280	261	1,551	1,305	4,711	1,746	21	348
8	−	373	1,188	136	1,181	1,520	4,406	1,645	21	473

STATION	YEAR	STAFF Supervisory and Wages (all Grades) No.	Paybill Expenses £	TOTAL RECEIPTS £	PASSENGER TRAIN TRAFFIC Tickets issued No.	Season Tickets No.	Receipts Passengers (including Season Tickets, etc.) £	Parcels £	Miscellaneous £	Total £
Chippenham Passenger	1903	68	4,613	18,792	106,639	*	13,046	2,774	2,972	18,792
	1913	49	3,842	26,017	121,045	*	14,865	2,878	8,274	26,017
	1923	55	10,007	39,390	137,138	947	24,364	3,413	11,613	39,390
	1924	56	9,822	47,627	139,313	925	25,949	3,627	18,051	47,627
	1925	55	9,980	56,803	145,192	823	25,547	4,222	27,034	56,803
	1926	55	9,543	50,055	134,253	638	23,414	3,969	22,672	50,055
	1927	55	9,953	50,011	144,805	640	25,076	4,376	20,559	50,011
	1928	55	9,727	45,105	144,783	610	24,962	4,745	15,398	45,105
	1929	56	9,620	43,865	149,937	601	24,028	4,675	14,982	43,685
	1930	55	9,889	46,933	141,176	599	23,469	4,517	18,947	46,933
	1931	53	9,166	37,568	127,748	523	20,884	4,048	12,636	37,568
	1932	52	8,738	35,238	118,359	558	19,316	3,540	12,382	35,238
	1933	51	8,503	31,209	108,325	592	18,366	3,867	8,976	31,209
Chippenham Goods	1903	*	*	38,866						
	1913	19	1,134	41,396						
	1923	18	3,057	51,408						
	1924	21	3,485	55,258						
	1925	21	3,523	56,752						
	1926	21	3,374	53,753						
	1927	22	3,426	56,389						
	1928	23	3,434	55,393						
	1929	23	3,309	51,889						
	1930	23	3,482	52,668						
	1931	21	3,229	45,231						
	1932	20	3,000	43,280						
	1933	19	3,061	39,022						
Corsham	1903	13	858	36,641	44,937	*	3,137	637	308	4,082
	1913	10	782	18,557	41,484	*	3,046	565	418	4,029
	1923	9	1,524	18,516	42,905	419	3,721	689	731	5,141
	1924	9	1,460	18,595	42,351	359	3,653	617	836	5,106
	1925	9	1,503	18,753	44,853	387	3,821	490	997	5,308
	1926	9	1,396	16,807	40,578	441	3,453	506	900	4,859
	1927	9	1,523	17,014	44,092	404	3,553	545	1,052	5,150
	1928	9	1,517	16,266	43,072	503	3,707	537	863	5,107
	1929	9	1,493	15,919	45,377	479	4,053	551	1,177	5,781
	1930	9	1,467	15,007	45,713	464	3,685	543	1,170	5,398
	1931	8	1,444	13,435	40,863	426	3,385	509	1,027	4,921
	1932	8	1,329	10,464	36,173	377	3,123	489	756	4,368
	1933	8	1,270	10,906	34,866	391	3,017	548	121	3,686
Box, Mill Lane Halt †	1930	Included With Box.		826	15,339	125	811	7	8	826
	1931			1,065	19,308	185	1,048	14	3	1,065
	1932			1,071	17,687	237	1,061	10	–	1,071
	1933			1,044	15,555	218	1,034	10	–	1,044
Box	1903	11	672	18,466	39,266	*	1,983	318	176	2,477
	1913	8	622	9,819	31,116	*	1,475	333	550	2,358
	1923	9	1,604	12,171	33,255	460	2,097	440	516	3,058
	1924	9	1,453	12,214	31,693	405	2,004	370	451	2,825
	1925	9	1,614	11,450	30,565	413	1,907	188	599	2,694
	1926	9	1,466	10,433	27,383	425	1,788	212	407	2,407
	1927	9	1,499	10,419	29,105	375	1,801	214	617	2,632
	1928	9	1,422	9,839	28,309	341	1,704	217	453	2,374
	1929	9	1,299	10,575	30,074	345	1,745	250	615	2,610
	1930	9	1,386	9,345	19,408	208	1,019	236	524	1,779
	1931	9	1,367	7,834	13,777	145	797	212	600	1,609
	1932	8	1,248	6,082	10,517	80	622	177	558	1,357
	1933	8	1,264	5,746	8,343	73	574	191	251	1,016
Bathford Halt		Opened	March	1929						
	1929			273	11,466	3	273	–	–	273
	1930	Included with Bathampton		347	15,095	16	347	–	–	347
	1931			315	14,665	11	315	–	–	315
	1932			315	13,731	17	315	–	–	315
	1933			320	13,380	23	320	–	–	320

* Not available   †Opened March 1930

GOODS TRAIN TRAFFIC										
Forwarded			Received							
Coal and Coke 'Charged'	Other Minerals	General Merchandise	Coal and Coke 'Charged'	Other Minerals	General Merchandise	Coal and Coke 'Not Charged' (Forwarded and Received)	Total Goods Tonnage	Total Receipts (excluding 'Not Charged' Coal and Coke)	Livestock (Forwarded and Received)	Total Carted Tonnage (included in Total Goods Tonnage)
Tons	Tons	Tons	Tons	Tons	Tons	Tons	Tons	£	Wagons	Tons
12	723	16,865	12,781	11,402	29,166	13,249	84,198	38,866	2,443	14,903
630	617	20,115	17,583	10,830	29,008	9,782	88,565	41,396	2,220	18,044
166	1,060	11,279	13,170	12,923	22,209	13,660	74,467	51,408	1,707	10,159
191	1,856	14,293	14,155	14,003	25,356	15,569	85,423	55,258	1,549	12,741
794	1,138	13,513	14,815	15,966	25,106	15,935	87,267	56,752	2,220	11,483
366	1,372	12,617	9,824	15,170	24,402	14,465	78,216	53,753	2,074	11,233
227	1,121	13,653	14,906	13,657	23,762	14,894	82,220	56,389	1,852	10,563
677	1,506	13,575	11,435	13,688	22,581	18,128	81,590	55,393	2,333	13,133
653	1,754	14,924	12,216	11,834	21,625	18,766	81,772	51,889	1,687	12,756
603	1,377	15,148	11,284	11,230	22,163	18,502	80,307	52,668	1,432	13,022
466	1,403	12,492	7,081	9,140	21,262	18,601	70,445	45,231	1,230	11,006
606	980	10,441	5,731	6,161	24,623	19,015	67,557	43,280	1,033	13,741
375	740	10,217	5,925	3,691	22,549	15,018	58,515	39,022	1,040	14,583
—	82,487	675	5,947	4,632	3,633	2,593	99,967	32,559	—	1,224
54	30,468	1,600	5,806	2,625	2,387	2,379	45,319	14,528	—	1,401
—	18,751	995	2,467	1,920	1,433	2,767	28,333	13,375	1	1,007
30	19,923	922	2,813	2,747	1,557	3,006	30,998	13,489	—	946
—	20,538	938	2,665	1,759	1,606	2,633	30,139	13,445	—	932
29	15,097	769	1,767	2,837	1,707	2,197	24,403	11,948	2	906
—	13,891	742	2,307	1,968	1,634	3,369	23,911	11,864	9	921
6	11,688	2,932	1,808	1,671	1,648	2,834	22,587	11,159	10	840
—	10,282	3,274	1,831	1,259	1,304	3,139	21,089	10,138	26	803
—	9,427	3,343	1,961	1,049	1,357	3,300	20,437	9,609	22	755
16	8,891	2,791	2,368	420	1,269	3,578	19,333	8,514	6	704
—	5,894	1,758	1,661	106	896	3,439	13,754	6,096	4	773
9	6,738	2,083	1,573	259	1,302	2,128	14,092	7,220	5	1,170
—	33,849	1,438	5,303	4,765	5,876	2,552	53,783	15,989	51	1,633
—	9,892	3,848	3,888	3,526	5,270	1,890	28,314	7,461	58	1,071
—	4,430	3,359	1,281	2,697	4,432	1,510	17,709	9,118	75	1,418
8	6,370	3,376	1,064	5,696	4,334	1,400	22,248	9,389	53	1,167
8	4,663	3,726	1,309	3,853	3,871	1,577	19,007	8,756	50	1,380
11	4,406	2,966	460	3,550	4,342	955	16,690	8,026	47	1,280
16	3,553	2,378	1,049	2,425	4,673	1,617	15,711	7,787	58	1,091
7	2,756	2,624	860	3,201	3,759	1,408	14,615	7,465	85	853
—	3,097	3,186	1,054	4,178	3,090	1,478	16,083	7,965	97	928
—	2,903	3,339	1,334	3,219	2,679	1,217	14,691	7,566	75	698
9	2,309	2,552	1,155	2,963	2,501	1,568	13,057	6,225	66	473
—	2,374	1,034	1,084	1,099	2,651	1,445	9,687	4,725	67	675
9	2,592	1,325	1,087	1,202	2,610	1,546	10,371	4,730	45	477

STATION	YEAR	STAFF		TOTAL RECEIPTS	PASSENGER TRAIN TRAFFIC						
							Receipts				
		Supervisory and Wages (all Grades)	Paybill Expenses		Tickets issued	Season Tickets	Passengers (including Season Tickets, etc.)	Parcels	Miscellaneous	Total	
		No.	£	£	No.	No.	£	£	£	£	
Bathampton	1903	7	457	2,287	35,117	*	1,004	132	7	1,143	
	1913	6	480	1,854	21,373	*	650	101	3	754	
	1923	8	1,346	3,540	19,531	78	764	103	4	871	
	1924	8	1,314	3,531	19,268	92	694	104	5	808	
	1925	8	1,346	3,629	22,236	125	838	101	6	945	
	1926	8	1,311	3,845	20,700	139	783	116	26	925	
	1927	7	1,277	4,206	24,551	150	883	99	4	988	
	1928	7	1,192	3,991	24,490	158	974	90	3	1,067	
	1929	7	1,161	4,189	21,884	135	817	76	10	903	
	1930	7	1,181	4,027	19,990	126	720	87	9	816	
	1931	7	1,117	3,566	19,342	117	724	69	4	797	
	1932	7	1,124	3,318	18,274	138	675	52	4	731	
	1933	7	1,141	3,679	16,801	259	773	65	−	838	
Bath Passenger	1903	76	4,621	84,160	405,577	*	66,584	10,861	6,715	84,160	
	1913	76	6,059	86,371	402,301	*	70,246	10,905	5,220	86,371	
	1923	84	13,788	153,872	470,378	5,103	131,628	15,453	6,791	153,872	
	1924	82	13,588	158,049	494,893	4,512	136,359	15,056	6,634	158,049	
	1925	77	13,238	157,412	528,938	5,599	135,072	15,310	7,030	157,412	
	1926	77	13,157	146,852	473,742	8,536	125,147	14,865	8,840	146,852	
	1927	79	13,556	153,566	485,874	9,719	129,786	15,798	7,982	153,566	
	1928	†79	†13,626	147,125	460,066	9,151	122,864	16,598	7,663	147,125	
	1929	†81	†13,566	133,847	387,867	7,362	110,342	15,711	7,794	133,847	
	1930	†80	†13,635	126,680	355,887	6,738	103,807	14,870	8,003	126,680	
	1931	†79	†12,952	114,661	304,022	6,049	92,537	14,448	7,676	114,661	
	1932	†76	†12,406	105,874	288,719	5,787	85,016	13,927	6,931	105,874	
	1933	†76	†12,347	103,250	274,976	5,610	82,996	13,604	6,630	103,250	
Bath Goods	1903	*	*	43,362							
	1913	64	4,690	53,433							
	1923	65	10,474	82,857							
	1924	61	10,259	80,450							
	1925	61	10,210	79,690							
	1926	61	9,775	75,320							
	1927	61	10,828	86,166							
	1928	60	9,832	80,936							
	1929	60	9,720	78,455							
	1930	60	9,923	75,268							
	1931	60	9,689	70,859							
	1932	57	8,866	57,448							
	1933	54	8,748	58,516							

* Not available   †Including Staff and Expenses from 1928

GOODS TRAIN TRAFFIC

Forwarded			Received							
Coal and Coke 'Charged'	Other Minerals	General Merchandise	Coal and Coke 'Charged'	Other Minerals	General Merchandise	Coal and Coke 'Not Charged' (Forwarded and Received)	Total Goods Tonnage	Total Receipts (excluding 'Not Charged' Coal and Coke)	Livestock (Forwarded and Received)	Total Carted Tonnage (included in Total Goods Tonnage)
Tons	Tons	Tons	Tons	Tons	Tons	Tons	Tons	£	Wagons	Tons
–	15	758	181	730	2,950	531	5,165	1,144	3	310
–	30	463	197	320	592	487	2,089	1,100	–	748
–	–	661	142	524	1,180	176	2,683	2,669	–	878
–	9	736	144	353	1,707	191	3,140	2,728	–	887
9	5	879	197	218	1,605	205	3,118	2,684	1	921
9	7	863	125	269	2,056	228	3,557	2,920	1	855
6	8	883	616	270	1,537	447	3,767	3,220	–	960
–	–	825	476	187	1,738	354	3,580	2,924	–	799
–	109	1,008	516	203	2,058	287	4,181	3,286	–	804
–	31	855	504	177	2,355	365	4,287	3,211	–	781
8	–	768	495	182	2,123	240	3,816	2,769	–	629
–	–	696	405	186	2,307	261	3,855	2,587	2	620
10	–	961	264	150	2,167	312	3,864	2,841	–	664
814	3,207	19,341	12,344	33,083	31,118	6,695	106,602	43,362	1,046	21,318
867	40	26,259	18,772	10,353	53,265	12,720	122,276	53,433	1,247	28,446
–	1,799	17,247	16,904	6,557	46,550	6,278	95,335	82,857	942	22,962
20	1,373	19,129	16,246	7,259	48,590	6,364	98,981	80,450	884	23,671
41	2,027	19,093	15,567	7,160	45,085	9,832	98,805	79,690	904	23,977
152	1,452	17,131	10,428	7,779	43,157	11,084	91,183	75,320	820	22,886
55	2,473	18,808	11,745	9,003	46,814	14,783	103,681	86,166	848	24,863
15	3,055	18,249	9,993	7,998	43,975	18,544	101,829	30,036	744	22,819
59	3,255	15,680	12,452	6,811	39,682	21,830	99,779	78,455	714	23,618
14	2,088	14,593	9,726	4,520	40,800	25,012	97,653	75,268	705	23,503
7	1,285	12,672	8,518	5,223	39,759	25,025	92,489	70,859	456	22,698
–	1,434	8,688	7,151	3,466	31,666	27,788	80,193	57,448	447	19,760
248	2,488	10,226	8,643	4,415	33,896	30,740	90,656	58,516	319	20,354

APPENDIX 7

CHIPPENHAM LOG, 22 JUNE 1963

Note that the departure times of trains are as from Chippenham unless otherwise stated. Details of local stopping services handled by DMUs, including the Calne branch, are not recorded.

3834 Up freight passed at 7.30 a.m.
5929 1C17 Sdn – Pz. 7.32 Down.
D7048 1C16 7.54 Up.
D7074 1A00 7.54 Down
6862 Down pick-up freight.
4653 Bristol–Chippenham freight.
9680 8.20 Trowbridge–Chippenham.
6974 Up parcels.
D7040 1A14 9.00 Up.
D7044 1B04 Down Bristolian.
D7010 1A30 10.00 Up.
9773 Freight to Calne.

82007 ECS for 1.12 p.m. Calne–WSM.
D7027 1A42 11.56 Up.
5038 11.56 Down arr. at 12.15 after loco failure.
5098 12.31 Down.
5986 12.50 Up Weymouth–Birmingham.
5929 1A49 12.56 Down.

4956 1.38 Down.
D7074 1.50 1B13 Down.
D7026 1A64 2.00 Up.
D7040 1B15 2.41.
6870 2.25 Weymouth.
9773 returning Calne freight.
D7050 1B17 Down.
D7044 1A74 4.00 Up.

6940 6.14 Up.
D839 1C86 6.30 Down.
4956 7.00 Down.
6970 6.50 Up.
D7073 1A33 7.02.
3804 Up ballast train.
7916 7.59 Up.
D7006 1B28 8.27 Down.
D1057 1A50 8.30 Up.

(Christopher Kent)

BIBLIOGRAPHY

BOOKS

Ahrons, E.L., *Locomotive & Train Working in the Latter Part of the Nineteenth Century*, Vol. 4, Cambridge, Heffer, 1952

Biddle, G. and Nock, O.S., *The Railway Heritage of Britain*, London, Michael Joseph, 1983

Bourne, J.C., *The History & Description of the Great Western Railway*, London, David Bogue, 1846

Bradshaw's Railway Guide, various years

Brooke, D., *The Railway Navvy*, London, Hutchinson, 1965

Chapman, W.G., *Track Topics*, London, GWR, 1935

Clark, R.H. and Potts, C.R., *An Historical Survey of Selected Great Western Railway Stations*, Vols 1 to 4, Oxford, OPC, 1976–85

Clew, K.R., *The Kennet & Avon Canal*, Newton Abbot, David & Charles, 1968

Clinker, C.R., *Register of Closed Passenger Stations & Goods Depots*, Weston-super-Mare, Avon-Anglia, 1988

Coleman, T., *The Railway Navvies*, Harmondsworth, Penguin, 1968

Cooke, R.A., *Track Layout Diagrams of the GWR & BR WR*, Sections 20 and 21, Harwell, Author, 1988 and 1987

Gale, T., *A Brief Account of the Making and the Working of the Great Box Tunnel*, Bath, Peach, 1884

GWR *Appendix to No. 4 Section of the Service Time Tables*, 1911 and 1931

Hateley, R., *Industrial Locomotives of Central Southern England*, Market Harborough, Industrial Railway Society, 1981

Leitch, R., *The Railways of Keynsham*, Long Sutton, Railway Correspondence & Travel Society, 1997

Leleux, S., *Brotherhoods Engineers*, Newton Abbot, David & Charles, 1965

Lyons, E., *An Historical Survey of Great Western Engine Sheds, 1947*, Oxford, OPC, 1974

Lyons, E. and Mountford, E., *An Historical Survey of Great Western Engine Sheds 1837–1947*, Oxford, OPC, 1979

MacDermot, E.T., Clinker, C.R. and Nock, O.S., *History of the Great Western Railway*, London, Ian Allan, 1964 and 1967

Maggs, C.G., *The GWR Bristol to Bath Line*, Stroud, Sutton Publishing, 2001

McCamley, N.J., *Secret Underground Cities*, Barnsley, Leo Cooper, 1998

Measom, C., *Official Guide to the Great Western Railway*, London, Griffin, Bohn, 1852

Platts, A., *A History of Chippenham*, Chippenham, Author, 1946

Railway Correspondence & Travel Society, *Locomotives of the Great Western Railway*, Vols 1 to 14, Long Stratton, RCTS, 1952–93

Robertson, K. and Abbott, D., *GWR: the Badminton Line*, Gloucester, Alan Sutton, 1988

Scott, M., *Discovering Widcombe & Lyncombe*, Bath, Widcombe Association, 1993

Searle, M.U., *Down the Line to Bristol*, London, Baton Transport, 1986

Sectional Appendix to the Working Time Table and Books of Rules and Regulations, Bristol Traffic District, BR, 1960

Sekon, G.A., *A History of the Great Western Railway*, London, Digby, Long, 1895

Simms, F.W., *Practical Tunnelling*, London, Hythe, 1896

Tunstall, J., *Rambles in Bath & District*, Bath, Peach, 1847

Victoria County History of Wiltshire, Vol. 4, London, OUP, 1959

Williams, F.S., *Our Iron Roads*, London, Bemrose & Son, 1883

Wroughton, J., *Bath in the Age of Reform*, Bath, Morgan, 1992

NEWSPAPERS & JOURNALS

Bath & Cheltenham Gazette, Bath Chronicle, Bath & County Graphic, Bath Herald, Bristol Gazette, Bristol Journal, British Railway Journal, The Builder, Engineering, Great Western Railway Journal, Railway Magazine, Wiltshire Independent.

INDEX

Page references that include illustrations are given in italics. Illustrated locomotives are listed under the entry 'locomotives'.